D0421788

The Vanishing Village

A DANISH MARITIME COMMUNITY

by
ROBERT T. ANDERSON
and
BARBARA GALLATIN ANDERSON

Seattle   University of Washington Press   1964

XAVIER UNIVERSITY LIBRARY
NEW ORLEANS, LA. 70125

Copyright © 1964 by the University of Washington Press
Library of Congress Catalog Card Number 64-12898
Manufactured by Vail-Ballou Press, Inc., Binghamton, N.Y.

118928

309.1
A549v

TO VICTOR T. ANDERSON AND STELLA I. ANDERSON

Preface

THIS is the history of a Danish maritime village as an anthropologist might see it. Its orientation is to social and cultural processes. Because of this orientation, only the first chapter attempts to deal thoroughly with the total history of the community, since detailed analysis requires documentation that can only be had for more recent times. Fortunately, one of the most exciting phases of sociocultural evolution took place during the twentieth century and can be reconstructed. Concentration is upon this latter phase.

The ethnological methods employed for the study varied with the period under analysis. For the contemporary community data were accumulated by direct observation, participant observation, and interviewing. The bulk of the information was derived from seventy-eight informants in the course of a year's residence, from July, 1956, to June, 1957. Of the forty-two women, twenty-five men, and eleven children interviewed, fifty-two reside in the old part of town, the principal focus of the study. The remainder were drawn from the new "Meadow Park" development section and from the villa quarter. Interviews varied widely in duration, averaging an hour and a half per meeting, and some informants were seen as many as a half-dozen times. Questionnaires, both structured and unstructured, were used to supplement data, and to uncover the fullest possible reservoir of information pertinent to the sphere of cultural change.

In reconstructing Dragor of the 1890's it was impossible to rely as heavily on informants, although thirteen were located and exhaustively interviewed. Two families very generously allowed the study of private diaries dating from the period, and Dragor's museum had documents, letters, and publications as well as material evidence which proved useful. In addition, some very pertinent local histories were invaluable. Above all Christian Nicolaisen, the postmaster of the community in the late nineteenth century, wrote a three-volume history of the island in which Dragor is given detailed consideration, and a former priest of the village, Mogens Strunge, has written graphically on its past.[1]

During the entire study, the local physician, Dr. Poul Dich, who by avocation interested himself greatly in the history of the local area and had written on it, was generous in his assistance as was the local priest, Mr. S. A. Andersen. Both were influential in opening many private doors and in encouraging informants to speak freely, often on subjects of considerable delicacy.

Special thanks for indispensable aid are due Mr. and Mrs. Kristen Arentoft, Mr. and Mrs. Harry Christofersen, Mr. and Mrs. Christian Jensen, Mr. and Mrs. U. Jørgensen, Mr. Einar Larsen, Mr. and Mrs. Egon Lauridsen, Mr. Poul Hoyers, Mrs. Else Stenersen, Mr. and Mrs. Erik Schødt, and Mr. and Mrs. Peder Taarnby.

Chief Inspector Holger Rasmussen of the National Museum in Copenhagen was a supportive friend and advisor during the year in Denmark. Professors Robert H. Lowie and George M. Foster of the University of California and Professor Edward Norbeck of Rice University were invaluable consultants in all phases of work. Professors André Leroi-Gourham, Jean Stoetzel, Georges Chabot, and Roger Bastid of the Sorbonne read earlier drafts. Our photographer was Professor Stanley V. Anderson of the University of California at Santa Barbara.

Above all we wish to thank the Dragorians who made this study possible by deep-rooted friendliness and through cooperation based on the charitable belief that an understanding of their history of change might be useful in solving man's problems elsewhere in this century of progress.

We are pleased to acknowledge generous financial support. The year of field study was financed by a Social Science Research Council Research Training Fellowship. Parts of the manuscript were first written when we were Postdoctoral Fellows of the National Science Foundation. The final volume was completed as

[1] For citations to the works of Christian Nicolaisen and Mogens Strunge see n. 1, Chapter One.

part of a larger project financed by a National Science Foundation research grant and during time made available by grants from the Danforth Foundation and the Mills College Faculty Research Fund.

Contents

Illustrations

The Vanishing Village

A DANISH MARITIME COMMUNITY

JUTLAND

COPENHAGEN
AMAGER IS.
SALTHOL
IS.
ST. MAGLEBY
DRAGOR

SEALAND

FUNEN

DENMARK

1: Region and Nation: Amager Island

DENMARK is a nation of some five hundred islands plus the peninsula of Jutland.[1] One of the many islands is Amager. Small (65 sq. km.) and flat, it is separated by a narrow strait from Copenhagen, located on Sealand, the largest of the Danish islands. In 1520 a colony of Dutch farmers moved onto this island of Amager. The roots of the colonization go back a few additional years to a royal love affair. While still crown prince, Christian II fell in love with Dyveke, an exile from North Holland whom he met during a sojourn in the Norwegian provinces. In 1513, after

[1] This chapter was published as "The Danish and Dutch Settlements on Amager Island: Four Hundred Years of Socio-Cultural Interaction." *American Anthropologist*, LX (August, 1958), 683–701. Recent historical data were collected in the field. Older historical data are taken from Louis Bobé, "Amager," in *Holland-Danmark*, I, edited by Knud Fabricius, *et al.* (Copenhagen: Jespersen og Pios, 1945); Christian Nicolaisen, *Dragørs Fortid og Fremme* (Copenhagen: Rasmussen og Olsens, 1887); Christian Nicolaisen, *Amagers Historie, bilagt med de vigtigste breve og aktstykker om øens forhold*, 3 vols. (Copenhagen: Nordisk [vol. 1] and Schous [vols. 2 and 3], 1907, 1909, 1915); Gunnar Olsen, "Landbruget," in *Holland-Danmark*, edited by Knud Fabricius, *et al.* (Copenhagen: Jespersen og Pios, 1945); Elna Mygdal, *Amagerdragter Vævninger og Syninger* (Danmarks Folkeminder Nr. 37) (Copenhagen: Schønbergske, 1932); Mogens Strunge, *Jernskiægs Amagerrim 1693* (Copenhagen: Levin og Munksgaard, 1935); Mogens Strunge, *De Thurah og Hans Amagerbog fra 1758* (Copenhagen: Levin og Munksgaard, 1936); J. P. Trap, *Kongeriget Danmark*, II, *Københavns Amt* (4th rev. ed.; Copenhagen: G. E. C. Gads, 1929); Jan Zibrandtsen, *Den Hollandske Kultur paa Amager* (Copenhagen: 1938).

3

ascending the throne, Christian brought Dyveke and her mother, known as Mother Sigbrit, to Copenhagen, giving them a house in the capital as well as a summer residence on Amager. Through his attachment to the daughter, Christian came under the influence of Mother Sigbrit, a forceful woman who had a hand in many events in his reign, including, it seems quite certain, the negotiations that brought immigrants to Amager from North Holland.

The Dutch were invited to settle in Denmark because their skill and advanced techniques in agriculture and dairying would enable them to supply the court and the capital with high quality vegetables, butter, and cheese. Mother Sigbrit was apparently quick to see that the island of Amager, flat, fertile, and convenient to Copenhagen, was well suited to Dutch techniques. And because it was the private property of the king, it could be made available. In 1515 Christian issued his earliest invitation to the Netherlands. In 1516 a few Dutchman came to Denmark, presumably to inspect personally the land being offered them. Late in 1520 the colony came, 184 people comprising twenty-four families.

In a letter of privileges granted in 1521, King Christian II gave the immigrants all of the island of Amager excepting the royal fishing camp at Dragor (Dragør) but including the neighboring island of Saltholm. The utility of the latter was limited by its seasonal inundation. Although much of Amager lay unused, the 736 Danish indigenes were told to turn over their farms to the newcomers. The situation, however, remained fluid for a number of years. Before all of the Danes were evacuated, Christian II was forced to flee the country and was replaced on the throne in 1523 by his uncle, Frederick I, who lacked special interest in the Dutch. In 1541, twenty years after the Dutch first came, the situation was crystallized by the issuance of a royal letter of protection which affirmed the Danish farmers' rights to their farms on northern Amager as well as their equal rights with the Dutch to use the meadows, chalk deposits, and fishing grounds of Saltholm. Many of the farms were returned to the original owners, and although in 1547 Frederick's successor, Christian III, reaffirmed the privileges of the Dutch essentially as they were originally given in 1521, the practical effect was that the immigrants were confined to the southern part of the island, leaving the northern part to the original inhabitants.

The center of the colony was ancient Søndre Magleby, a village of about twenty farms. Renamed Store Magleby (Dutch, Grote Maglebeu), it was much changed in order to satisfy the newcomers' needs for land distribution and was completely rebuilt after suffering destruction in the Count's Feud (1533–36).

The Immigrant Dutch Amagerians

The land was the private property of the colonists. As stated in the original letter of privileges and reaffirmed by Christian III, the Dutch were free to divide the land among themselves, to sell it, and to give it in inheritance, all according to Dutch customs. The only restriction on ownership, other than the requirement to pay taxes, was that if a family died out completely the land was to revert to the crown, but with the proviso that it was then to be auctioned off by the village head to the highest bidder, who was always a Dutchman. In accordance with these privileges, the twenty-four families divided the land into twenty-four farms of from thirty-five to forty acres each. The rest of the land was used in common; each farmer had the use of grazing areas in proportion to the amount of his land kept under the plow, the total amount of land available to each of the original farms being approximately 135 acres. With the passage of time and the division of farms by inheritance and sale, the land became parceled into many small plots, a single farmer having as many as thirty or forty separate strips. The farms also became unequal in size and value.

The royal privileges included the right to local independent government according to Dutch customs. The communal government thus ordained was under the leadership of a *schout* or *schultus,* who was elected for life by the adult farm owners and was under oath only to the representative (*lensmand,* later *amtsmand*) of the king. The schout was chairman of the village council, consisting of himself and seven men called *scheppens.* Scheppens were elected for one-year terms every New Year's Day when a village meeting was held. In this meeting it was also customary to read aloud accounts of public affairs and to vote upon village ordinances, suffrage being the prerogative of the male farm owners.

The village had its own law court, also patterned upon Dutch practices. The nine members were the schout, the seven scheppens, and a secretary. The secretary, also elected by the villagers, was generally the man who became schout when the incumbent died. The court judged in all legal cases except those where the punishment would be "neck or hand," in which case the king judged. Later, the king's vassal (*lensmand*) came to function as an appellate judge, and in 1576 he appointed two royal chancellors to undertake a revision of the Dutch laws in view of some dissatisfaction that existed with their fairness. Later still, the Dutch laws were replaced successively by the Sealand Lawbook, the Jutland Lawbook, and "Christian V's Danish Law," but the Dutch were permitted to retain deviating rules in a number of areas, as well as their old form for holding court. Court met four times a year—New Year's Day, Easter, St. John's Day, and St. Michael's Day. As symbol of his judgeship, the schout carried a long white staff, and on opening the court in the name of God, the king, and the congregation, he drew three crosses on the table with chalk, to be erased when court adjourned.

The church in Store Magleby, which had formerly belonged to the cathedral in Copenhagen, was part of the property given the Dutch when they settled on Amager. The first priest was probably one of the original Dutch settlers. Subsequent replacements were speakers of Low German, mostly brought in from the Duchy of Holstein. The parish was independent of the Sealand bishop and exempt from the so-called church tithe and priest tithe, paying only the third of the three divine payments, the king's tithe. In 1560 the king allocated his tithe to the Sealand see, very likely to reimburse the bishop for the loss of income sustained by the king's generosity to the colonists. In 1672 the congregation was also exempted from paying the king's tithe, in return for taking upon themselves all expenses for church, parsonage, priest's farm, and school.

The school may date from the earliest settlement. It was administered by the priest, who was probably also the schoolteacher. The first mention of a schoolmaster is not until around 1640, when it was noted that, in addition to a regular annual salary, he was entitled to money offerings made by the women at infant baptismal ceremonies. A knowledge of reading, writing, and arithmetic was important in this community where most adult men had active roles in communal administration.

The town treasury consisted of a large locked chest in the

charge of the schout and, possibly, the secretary. This chest functioned as the village bank. It held not only the village funds but also the fortunes of the inhabitants, including money inherited by minors.

Funds came into the public treasury from payments made for the use of communal properties and facilities. Such payments were made by those who grazed cattle on Saltholm or dug its chalk, by the men who leased and ran the Dutch windmill, by any family that had a new grave dug in the cemetery, by the men who fished for eels, and by others. Royal taxes and assessments were levied on the community as a whole, the responsibility for payment falling upon the schout. Since the village chest always contained sufficient funds, it was never necessary to charge local taxes. On the contrary, income from eel fishing alone appears to have been enough to pay the yearly land tax (*landgilde*), and sometimes there was so much money left over that it was divided among the members of the community. The village was often able to make loans to the inhabitants of the Danish villages of northern Amager against mortgages on land, interest and sometimes land secured by foreclosing mortgages augmenting the wealth of the Dutch community.

The expenses of the community were first of all a money tax (*landgilde*) and guest duty (*gæsteriafgift*), set at 300 marks by Christian III and later changed to 100 kurantdaler. In 1547 it was further demanded that the castle secretary (*slotsskriveren*) in Copenhagen be provided with root crops and onions to meet the needs of the castle and the court; this obligation was probably regarded as a substitute for villeinage labor (*hoveri*), from which the Dutch had been exempted in the privileges letter of 1521. The Dutch were also originally exempt from transportation duty (*ægt*), but under Christian III they were required to perform it on the king's behalf for the royal vassal (*lensmand*) in Copenhagen. Set at twenty-four "pantry-trips" (*fadebursrejser*) a year, it only amounted to one trip for each farm. In 1541 the right to free and exclusive use of Saltholm was rescinded and the Dutch had to share use and expenses with the Danish Amagerians, the yearly cost being forty Jochumsdaler (160 marks), plus 200 loads of chalk; the Dutch paid two fifths and the Danes three fifths. In the 1660's these charges were replaced by an assessment according to the amount of land held under cultivation (*hart-*

korn), and gradually they disappeared completely. An extra tax, which soon became a regular annual expense, was 40 rigsdaler a year, to which were added taxes on grain and pork as well as money subscriptions at the time of the Swedish wars at the end of the seventeenth century. Those earning interest on loans paid the throne 2.5 per cent a year on this income. Finally, there were other smaller communal expenses such as bridge assessments, customs and excise, and payment for eel-fishing rights. The village did not pay the priest tithe or church tithe and was exempted from the king's tithe as well after 1672. For home defense in later years the Dutch were not required to quarter soldiers but did have to provide boatmen for the fleet, thirty or forty being demanded on some occasions.

The Indigenous Danish Amagerians

In the early period of the Dutch colony there were approximately ninety farms in the Danish parish, each leased directly from the king. Generally the right of usufruct lasted for the life of the farmer and his wife, although some farms were given to father and son or to mother and son for as long as one of them lived and continued to pay the land tax. On the death of the lessee a new letter of life tenure (*livsbrev*) had to be obtained; it was most commonly given to a son or son-in-law in return for the promise to pay a renewal charge (*indfæstningssum*) in addition to the annual rent.

The farmers in the Danish villages were subordinate to the king's vassal in Copenhagen's castle. The king's vassal had almost unlimited authority in virtually every aspect of daily life, including farm management, fees and taxes, and villeinage. However, the farmers rarely saw the lensmand, for he was represented in turn by the circuit sheriff (*ridefogden*), who directly supervised the area, appeared in court in law cases such as tax or lease disputes, and on the whole represented the king's vassal and the king. In each village, subservient to the circuit sheriff, was a local sheriff (*foged*) or alderman (*oldermand*), generally one of the biggest farmers in the area. It appears that the alderman was elected for life by the villagers, subject to the sanction of the king's vassal. It was his job to see to it that the town ordinances were kept, that the farmers worked without complaint or disturbance, and that problems which occurred were, if possible, resolved without resorting to lengthy and expensive court proceedings. The alderman also assigned farmers their turns in transportation duty, road corvées, and work on other public projects, on the whole carrying out the will of the crown and the royal vassal. In return he was freed from certain extra taxes, transportation duty, and public work.

When the Dutch came, the old Amager judicial district (*birk*) was divided; the Dutch became independent and the Danes came under a new jurisdiction, the Taarnby district court (*birkething*), functioning under the royal vassal and headed by a court sheriff (*thingfoged*). The latter, at first one of the district's most important farmers, was later called district sheriff (*birkefoged*), and instead of a farmer became a city man trained in law and governmental administration. The position required ability to read and write, which was uncommon among Danish farmers at that time, as well as familiarity with the old laws and with the legal rules and orders of the king and the council of the kingdom (*rigets raad*). He was assisted by the court secretary (*thingskriveren*), also trained in law. Both district sheriff and court secretary had to sign all judgments, decisions, and ordinances. The court met on Fridays in the Amager village of Taarnby and consisted of twelve jurors (*thingmænd* or *stokkemænd*) in addition to the district sheriff, sitting as judge (*birkedommer*), and the secretary. To be a juror was a royal duty divided among the older villagers; there were generally two from each village. The court had jurisdiction even in cases concerning "honor and life," but the authority of the judge became more and more absolute until the jurors had no influence in decisions. The farmers responded by neglecting their duty so that nonlandholding farm laborers (*husmænd*) came to be taken as permanent jurors in return for having their houses freed of taxes and royal burdens. Around 1700 the number of jurors was reduced to nine. The original court sheriffs were paid partly from the fines collected and partly in exemption from the land tax and most of the other burdens common to tenant farmers. In 1578 it was ordered that each farm in the district was to give a certain amount of "judge-grain" to the sheriff, but this was soon replaced with a money assessment amounting to two marks from each farm; although many were in arrears in their payments, the total sum due the judge in the seventeenth century was around 100 sletdaler, a rather good wage for that time. The court secretary was paid out of the money collected in fines. Judgments could be appealed to Sealand's parliament (*landsthing*) as a superior court when it was a matter of life, honor, or property. Such cases were common, since the court was strict and the offenses included fornication and adultery, fighting, "neglecting the court," holding a big wedding, and illegal sale of liquor. Many of the cases concerned extramarital sexual affairs, which were severely punished. According to a law of 1558, adultery was punished the first time with loss of nonreal property and money to the last farthing, the second time with loss of all property including real estate, and the third time with decapitation for the man and drowning for the woman. A man guilty of defloration of a virgin (*jomfrukrenkeri*) had to pay nine marks to the woman's guardian plus eight skilling grot to the court. On Amager as a whole, one or two cases of sexual misconduct (*lejermaalssager*) were generally tried each year. Most of the offenders were Dutchmen, who had been made subject to similar proscriptions on sexual conduct during the reign of Christian IV (1588–1648).

Taarnby church, like that of Store Magleby, had been an annex of the cathedral in Copenhagen. In 1474, before the Dutch colonization, the two Amagerian churches and the cathedral were taken from the pope and put under the jurisdiction of the university; the income from the churches was to provide wages for university teachers, who in turn were to hold church services or have them performed by a vicar. Apparently the crown had a superior right, since the churches were given in fief to the secretary of the castle (*slotsskriver*) in Copenhagen. Oftentimes the king obtained money by selling rights to church income and priest tithe, and the buyer then had the responsibility of providing a curate for the church. Following this custom, Taarnby church came under the jurisdiction of the university again in 1542, remaining there during the following centuries. The university had the right to appoint the priest for Taarnby parish, which had economic importance for the university faculty in providing a place of retirement for old professors. The congregation seldom had a word in the choice of their pastor, in spite of the church ordinance of 1539 which made free choice a legal right. Indeed, they usually did not even have a chance to hear him preach before he was called to his post.

Without a school before the 1700's, only a few of the farmers obtained any education for their children other than the teaching of the catechism by the priest after Sunday church services.

The Danish Amagerians were not land-bound serfs. On the contrary, in order to retain their farms they were subject to various taxes and assessments. The land tax was originally eight barrels of barley for each farm, but was later increased by two barrels of oats. Guesting expenses were levied on the villages as wholes, and amounted to approximately one fourth of a cow, one sheep or pig or two lambs, one goose or four hens or one daler in money from each farm every year. It is not known when these payments were changed to money, but the old rules were still in force around 1700. The tithe, not literally a tenth of the farmer's crops, was divided into three parts—king's tithe, church tithe, and priest tithe—and the amount of each was determined independently, varying according to the harvest. The king often leased rights to his tithe, and thus in 1560 he gave the Taarnby king's tithe to the bishop of Sealand, probably as a replacement of the loss sustained by the bishopric when the church was given to the university. At first the amount of villeinage which could be demanded was unlimited, and the Danish men were sometimes required to work daily during sowing, harvesting, and plowing seasons to the detriment of their own farm livelihood. In response to a complaint in 1529, the king set a maximum to the amount of work that could be demanded; the farmer had the right to be released from more than the maximum amount in return for paying one-half lødemark. In 1624 complete freedom from villeinage could be purchased for 300 speciedaler a year for the parish (four rigsdaler per farm), which was more than the Dutch paid in land tax for their whole parish. Exemption from villeinage did not include freedom from transportation duty, which, however, did not become oppressive until after the inauguration of the absolute monarchy in 1660. In 1627, for example, each of eighty Danish farmers was required to bring two loads of firewood to the court in Copenhagen. In addition to these permanent annual taxes, assessments were made which themselves often became permanent. During the long war with Sweden in the 1560's the government added special assessments in money and provisions and required the inhabitants to quarter soldiers. The extra tax or land help (*landehjælp*) of one daler from each farmer soon became a regular yearly expense, and under Christian IV it was doubled and tripled, with the addition of a grain tax, a pork tax, and, in 1646, a copper and tin tax. During armament for the Swedish war of 1658–60 there were a number of new taxes such as a cattle tax of one mark a head and a monthly contribution in money, a defense tax of twenty speciedaler from each farm, an increase in land help, pork tax, and grain tax. Finally, under Christian V, these taxes were unified by assessing a single tax according to the amount of land under cultivation (*hartkornskontribution*).

Danish and Dutch Amagerians Compared

With the settlement of the Dutch in the southern part of Amager, the island became the habitat of two distinct societies, each with its own culture. In their own eyes and in the eyes of their contemporaries, the sociocultural differences were of considerable magnitude and importance. The Dutch farms were privately owned and could be sold or inherited, subject only to the payment of taxes and assessments. The Danish farmers were the king's tenants, with only life-time leases. The Dutch community was governed by locally elected representatives according to Dutch procedural form and law (later, Danish law codes with allowances for Dutch practices). The Danes were governed by outsiders according to Danish law codes, their locally elected representatives acting only to enforce decisions made outside of the community. The Dutch lived under pronounced, voluntary communalism, while the Danes functioned as individuals except when forced by the government to act as a body. The Dutch owned their own church, chose their own Low German-speaking priest, and followed Dutch Protestant ritual. The Danes worshipped in a church belonging to the University of Copenhagen under a priest chosen independently of their wishes, according to Danish Protestant ritual. The Dutch supported their own church and minister. The price paid for religion by the Danes went to powers outside of the community. The Dutch had public schools. The Danes waited approximately two centuries before their children could get an elementary education. The Dutch, like the Danes, were subject to land tax, guesting duty, transportation duty, and special assessments, but the land tax was levied on the village as a whole and continued to be based upon a community of twenty-four farms. In addition, they were free of villeinage, which greatly oppressed the Danes.

Dutch economy differed from Danish in its emphasis upon dairy-ing, horse breeding, eel-fishing, and vegetable cultivation as op-posed to grain farming. All of these differences were epitomized in the view of contemporaries by the possession of mutually un-intelligible languages, different types of clothing, differences in houses and furnishings, and different customs in the celebration of holidays and personal events such as engagements and wed-dings.

Social intercourse was limited almost entirely to meetings re-sulting from spatial propinquity, the major exception being those instances in which Danish farmers mortgaged their farms to the Dutch. Socializing was kept to a minimum, and each sought out its own. The Dutch did not permit intermarriage; no Dane could be brought into Store Magleby and any Dutchman who married out was no longer considered a member of the community and was not allowed to participate in village affairs or to enjoy the villagers' special rights and privileges.

Ethnic Acculturation: The Sixteenth
and Seventeenth Centuries

For the first two centuries the Dutch increased in wealth and numbers. The original twenty-four families which established the colony in 1520 had become approximately seventy-five families in 1600, eighty in 1615, and one hundred and thirty in 1650. In 1651 twenty families moved to the island of Sealand on the other side of Copenhagen to found the colony of New Amager. The plague of 1654 and the contemporaneous Swedish war reduced the pop-ulation temporarily. Thirty farms and houses were abandoned, most of the farms supporting two or more families. By 1688, however, the population had increased again to ninety-nine fam-ilies in Store Magleby and thirty in New Amager.

The Danes, depressed to begin with, sank lower and lower into poverty under tax burdens, assessments, and villeinage. Soon after arriving the Dutch took over the two farms in Dragor, "the king's fishing camp" south of Store Magleby. In 1547, and again in 1574, royal permission was obtained to lease farms in the Danish villages, and the subsequent infiltration of the Dutch into the Danish parish increased at an accelerated pace. By the time of the wars which preceded the absolute monarchy in 1660, one fourth of the Danish land was in Dutch hands. During the early decades of the absolute monarchy the economic position of the Danes deteriorated rapidly; by 1680 the Amager Dutch averaged 3.5 horses or cattle to every hectare of land, while the Amager Danes averaged only 1.5. During this recession many Danes were forced off their farms into the land-laborer or worker class, and the farms were invariably taken over by the Dutch. In the prewar period may cases occurred in which the Dutch loaned money to the Danes and the creditors received ownership or usufruct of the land. After the war, in order to get the national economy on its feet as rapidly as possible, the king overlooked the fact that such farms were taken over without lease or payment to the crown, thus bringing life leases to a de facto end at the same time that a fifty-year period was inaugurated during which the land tax was not demanded. By the time the land tax was required again in 1708, much of the Danish farm land was in the hands of the Dutch.

The Dutch farmers came into positions of influence and power in the Danish towns. In 1672 the sheriffs of Tømmerup and Ullerup were Dutchmen, and by 1691 Dutch officials were also to be found in Maglebylille and Sundbyvester. By 1718 almost one third of the farmers in the Danish towns were Dutchmen who had taken over Danish farms either completely or in part as creditors, or had leased the farms from the crown. All of the large farms, in particular, were in Dutch hands.

Some of the Dutch worked the Danish lands as part of their own farms, while others moved to the new farms. All, however, continued to regard themselves as belonging to the mother village and for the most part managed to avail themselves of its privileges, especially with respect to permanent ownership of property and freedom from villeinage. In cases where Dutch were elected officials of Danish villages, it was because of their influence with the authorities deriving from their wealth and reputation for dependability and punctuality, and not because they had amalgamated with the Danes. In social life they kept as much as possible to the Dutch community, speaking Dutch and avoiding the Danes in daily life, regarding the latter as economically, socially, and intellectually inferior. Endogamy was a strict rule, and in the seventeenth century the king's permission was frequently sought to marry within the third degree of kinship; permission was always given in return for a judgment in favor of the poor, generally a hospital, although sometimes the king appropriated one half of the sum for himself. Nor would the Dutch permit their children to work for Danes, not even, it was held, if it were for the most important man in the kingdom. In addition to guarding their social and cultural integrity, the Dutch retained their special relationship to the royal house, the basis for their prosperity, by always being prompt in payments due the crown and by continuing to supply the capital and the court with their desirable products. Unique in their way of life and protected by the royal house, they stoutly insisted that they were not peasants (*bønder*) but "the King's Amagerians."

In contrast to their conservative neighbors, the Danes changed and came more and more to follow the Dutch way of life. In particular, they adopted the Dutch economy, learning to cultivate vegetables and to emphasize dairying, horse breeding, and eel fishing. Every Wednesday and Saturday all Amagerians carted their produce to the market at Amager Square in Copenhagen. Before the coming of the Dutch mostly fish were sold, but the Dutch created a reputation for fine vegetables, cheese, and buttermilk, and became especially known for their sweet cupbutter (*"søde koppesmør"*) which was sold to "gentlemen and bishops." The market constituted the most important source of money income for Amagerians, and the Danes began to capitalize on the success of the Dutch by offering similar products for sale. In order to do this, it was found advantageous to present themselves as Dutchmen, and by the seventeenth century it was customary for them to wear a variant of the Dutch national dress. Although not able to obtain the special prerogatives of communal government, land tenure, and villeinage exemption held by the Dutch, they did adopt at least one legal custom; in 1686 royal permission was received to use the Dutch rules of inheritance which divided property equally between sons and daughters, rather than the Danish rules which gave twice as much to a son as to a daughter. By the last half of the seventeenth century the Danes were clearly borrowing traditions out of a pure desire to be Dutch undiluted by obvious economic motivation; for example, they adopted the Shrovetide (*fastelavn*) celebration of the immigrants, even though they were not able to match the rich display of the latter. Finally, there was an important but poorly documented diffusion of the Dutch propensity for steadfast hard work, initiative, and reliability.

Relations between Dane and Dutchman were not free of conflict. As already noted, the indigenous farmers objected to expulsion from the island by Christian II in 1520 and succeeded in retaining or regaining much of their original territory, primarily under the protection of King Frederick I. In subsequent decades the outstanding trouble spot was Dragor, the royal Danish fishing village on the southern, Dutch part of the island. In 1520 the village, with two farms and a small fishing population, was no longer the important center it had been in the late Middle Ages when the Hansa League flourished in the Baltic. But during the sixteenth and seventeenth centuries its population grew steadily. On the one hand, Dutchmen came. The two farms of the village were leased by the king to Dutch farmers. In addition, the Store Magleby village government financed expansion and improvement of the harbor, thereby gaining rights to participation in shipping, fishing, and ship salvage; this resulted in the influx of many young Dutchmen, especially from families with more sons than the paternal farm could support. On the other hand, Danes immigrated from Sealand and the larger Sound area, coming to fish, salvage, and participate in the small-scale shipping of produce, firewood, and building materials.

The Dutch acquired political control of Dragor. Around 1600, when Hansa trade no longer necessitated a customs agent in the village, the job was given by the king to the schout of inland Store Magleby, who thus came to function as the supreme local authority (*foged*) in both villages. When Dragor later became larger, the schout got royal permission to appoint a deputy sheriff (*underfoged*) as resident chief of the harbor village, and a fellow Dutchman was always chosen.

While the Dutch Dragorians profited from this arrangement, the Danish did not. The latter were forced to share the obligations of the residents of Store Magleby, such as contributing to the payment of the Dutch land tax, without receiving the corresponding privileges; for example, they had no part in the commons, not even enough to tether a goose. In the long-continued dispute, sole recourse was to the king. Standing before the throne in 1674, the Dutch pleaded that the two communities, always united in the past, should continue to form parts of a single Church parish and politicolegal district. In spite of its basis in an incorrect statement of local history, the plea was upheld. Although there is no record of violence, Dragorian Danes continued to complain during succeeding decades, but as long as the Dutch enjoyed the special benevolence of the king, complaints were in vain and grumbling was the only solace.

Folk Amalgamation: The Eighteenth and Nineteenth Centuries

Between 1700 and 1720 Denmark was at war with Sweden, and as in previous Dano-Swedish wars, Amager suffered greatly; it was overrun and destroyed by armies, and drained of all resources to supply the besieged capital. The disaster of the prolonged war increased when the Black Plague struck in 1711, leaving half of the island's inhabitants dead and as many as two thirds in two of the Danish villages. This time the Dutch did not have the resiliency they had displayed in responding to past disasters, no doubt because of the royal act of 1717 which ended their special privilege of a permanent land tax assessed on Store Magleby on the basis of the original twenty-four farms. A number of the farms in both the Danish and the Dutch parish were left uninhabited in 1711, and even after 1750 there was still frequent mention of abandoned farms (øde gaarde).

The Dutch no longer enjoyed superior economic position; they had lost special privileges. And developments following the introduction of the absolute monarchy had resulted in a de facto end to life-time limits on farm ownership in the Danish parish; Danish property ownership now also included the right to sell and inherit with freedom from taxation on property transfer. In addition, the Danes had adopted the profitable farm economy of their neighbors.

The Dutch who suffered these changes in the second decade of the eighteenth century were reluctant to give up their sociocultural solidarity, but they were now fighting a losing battle against many of their own younger generation as well as against the Danes, who had ceased to be socioeconomic inferiors. In 1731 a Danish priest was called to work at Store Magleby church in addition to the Dutch priest, so that church services could now be offered in both languages, and in 1735 the first Danish-language wedding ceremony was held. The biggest break in the ethnic barrier came in 1758 when the schout of Store Magleby married the daughter of a well-known and respected Dane, the sheriff (*foged*) of the Danish town of Sundbyvester. The first sanctioned marriage of a Dutchman to a Dane, it was followed the next year by the marriage of the secretary of Store Magleby to another Danish girl from Sundbyvester. Before long, Dutch and Dutch-mixed elements dominated the whole island. In the 1770's half of the farms in the Danish parish were in Dutch hands and only five farmers were not in an "in-law" relationship with the Dutch.

In eighteenth century Dutch homes, people still spoke their own language, which by then was a mixture of Dutch, Low German, and Danish. For some time the men had been able to speak Danish; from the first they had known enough to deal in the Copenhagen market place and from an early period they had been forced to use Danish in law cases which came before the king or his vassal, as well as in other communications with the court. Yet, in law cases of a purely local nature, Dutch was used. The communal laws of 1711 were written in Dutch, and school and church functions were conducted in Dutch. In 1788 the Dutch priest issued a schoolbook in Low German, and the Dutch songbook, authorized in 1715, was still in use around 1800. By then, however, many people in the community spoke only Danish. When new communal laws were drawn up in 1811, they were written in Danish, and in the same year Dutch ceased to be used in church services. In 1818 the special jurisdiction of the Store Magleby court was revoked and the Dutch came under the Danish court system.

Some adults of the mid-nineteenth century attempted to perpetuate the Dutch language. A traveler in 1846 described a family in which the old farmer wrote a Dutch glossary for his son's Danish wife. But it was a hopeless fight against the younger generation, which could see no advantage to speaking Dutch rather than Danish.

With intermarriage, loss of language, and loss of unique forms of communal organization, the Dutch merged with their Danish neighbors. The result was neither a Dutch nor a Danish culture, but an Amager culture—strongly Danish, but differing from the rest of Denmark in a number of ways. Above all, Amagerians had their own form of economy, adapted to the contemporary market by increasing specialization in vegetables and the development of flower cultivation (especially tulips and carnations) at the expense of fishing and dairying. They had their own dress which, though changed considerably from its prototype in Holland, still distinguished the King's Amagerians from other Danes. The Scandian dialect of Danish spoken on the island had acquired words and sounds from Dutch, including a certain singing tone in the vocals. Details of housing and furnishing, such as the so-called Amager shelf, were distinctive features, as were holiday activities such as rolling and throwing eggs at Easter time, eating "bag porridge" at Christmas, and ceremonially riding the rounds of the farms on horseback at Shrovetide. Amagerians were known for their fine products, for their propensity for industriousness, and for reliability. Amager culture of the nineteenth century, an amalgam of Dutch and Danish proudly shared by all regardless of ethnic background, was unique enough to set the islanders off in contemporary eyes as the "Amager Dutch," purveyors of the best cabbages and vegetables in the realm.

Urban Assimilation: The Twentieth Century

The means of communication with Copenhagen changed radically in the 1900's. For centuries roads were maintained by the farmers themselves; the inhabitants of each town formed corvées, and their work was supervised by local aldermen and subject to inspection by the king's vassal and his circuit sheriff. Under this arrangement roads were narrow, the surfaces deeply rutted in summer and winter and muddy bogs in spring and fall. The situation was not improved in 1790, when toll was charged. Half of the money collected went to Amager residents and the other half to the state for road maintenance, but half of the toll was not sufficient for repairs. This resulted in vociferous complaints in the 1830's and a change in organization in 1840, when road care became the responsibility of a state agency. During the rest of the nineteenth century the roads were improved, and in the twentieth century the main roads were given an asphalt surface.

When the Dutch first came to the island it was connected with the capital only by a ferry. In the first half of the seventeenth century a small footbridge was built which Amagerians used in the transportation of goods in handcarts, and around 1660 this bridge was expanded and strengthened to accommodate horse-drawn wagons. In 1686 a second bridge was built, although most Amagerians continued for a long time to use the older one. These bridges, since rebuilt several times, are still the only dry connections with Sealand and the outside world.

Around 1600 Christian IV erected a gate on the island through which all travelers to the capital had to pass, and from that period until about 1850 it was the means by which all traffic was controlled; it levied a toll on market goods and denied passage during the night hours. Over poor roads and through this gate, centuries of Amagerians drove wagons to market on Wednesdays and Saturdays, but otherwise seldom ventured from their island. Even on these twice-weekly trips, however, they rarely had cause to go beyond the marketplace (*Amagertorv*), and intercourse with Copenhageners was limited to commercial dealings. Urban influence on Amagerian culture was minimal.

Both the city and the means of communication changed. The population of Copenhagen, which was about 10,000 in 1500, grew to be 102,000 in 1801, 477,000 in 1901, and about one million in 1951. In the 1890's bicycles came into use as a means of communication which all could afford. In 1907 a railroad was built along the island to offer regular, although somewhat expensive, transportation to the capital. The growing city began to expand across the bridges and onto the northern part of the island, where some farms gave way to suburban residences, and small summer villas were built along the beaches. However, most Amagerians were little affected. Their daily life continued much as before, and the most notable change was the disappearance of the Amager costume. In the 1880's the last man died who wore this distinctive garb; women ceased to wear it after the turn of the century except on holidays and to family celebrations, and since 1940 it has become rare even on these occasions. In part this was the result of pride attaching to the wearing of city clothes, but it was also argued by those adopting the new styles that the old were prohibitively expensive and very uncomfortable.

Quite different was the change that took place after World War II. By that time the need for housing was acute in the capital, since the population had skyrocketed during the war years when it had been impossible to build residences. Because of modern developments in communication, it proved practical to meet this need by the construction of suburban communities on Amager.

The hour-long bicycle trip from Dragor or Store Magleby to Copenhagen was not considered too long for daily commuting. In addition, the bus and streetcar, replacing the train, provided regular and dependable transportation at rates reasonable enough for the average commuting laborer or white-collar worker. The postwar years also witnessed a large increase in the number of motor bikes, motor scooters, and motorcycles, especially after 1950. Automobiles, however, remain a luxury enjoyed by few and are of significance for daily commuting primarily for the professional classes.

Amagerians were suddenly and dramatically urbanized. Much farm land was converted into residential developments or into the new international airport. The whole of the northern and central part of the island and many areas in the south became thickly populated. Of the remaining farms, many changed from truck gardening to modern hot-house cultivation, but still found it difficult to make a living because of the high taxes assessed since agricultural land became so valuable for suburban development. Influenced by their new neighbors, the Amager Dutch now look to Copenhagen for entertainment and large-scale shopping. Their young people and displaced adults commute to easy jobs in the city and are not forced to stay with the hard and now ill-paid work of farming.

The meeting of urbanites and islanders occurred without overt hostility or violence. Property disagreements were settled in the law courts, and occasional disgruntled Amagerians bemoaned the loss of a cherished way of life. On the whole, however, there is little evidence of significant individual maladjustment or interpersonal difficulties related to urbanization, no doubt owing to the nature of the Copenhagen patterns of behavior. The rapid growth of the city has been largely the result of immigration from the Danish countryside, with few non-Danish participants. Although the city is large (one million), the country as a whole is small (about four million) and has a relatively homogeneous rural culture. Growing primarily by immigration from the agricultural hinterland, the city represents a continuing compromise between urban ways and Danish rural culture which could be accepted by the Amagerians with a minimum of friction.

People still farming differ but slightly from other Danish farmers. Some still emphasize vegetable crops and flowers, but otherwise little of Amager culture remains. The young people have given up the local accent for the Copenhagen dialect. Unique Amager foods are rarely served. Indeed, the Shrovetide ritual is the only practice which still clearly marks the people as Amagerians. On the two Mondays of Shrovetide, when they wear high silk hats and corduroy vests and ride their decorated horses, they are following an old tradition which delights them and the many urban spectators as well. However, interest is waning, and the horses have largely been replaced by tractors. In 1956 the villagers rode only one of the two Mondays, and since the airport expanded into more farms in 1958, the number of available horses has declined even more. The Amagerian is virtually extinct, and the island belongs to Copenhageners.

A Summing-Up

Three phases of culture change are discernible in the history of Amager island. In the first phase, lasting about two centuries (the sixteenth and seventeenth), the cultural integrity of the Dutch as a separate and distinct ethnic group persisted unimpaired. In fact, the Danish Amagerians adopted many Dutch traits. This phase of change is termed acculturation since the trend was for these adjacent cultures to become more similar.

In the second phase of culture change, which also lasted two centuries (the eighteenth and nineteenth), acculturation ultimately resulted in a single culture which was neither Dutch nor Danish but Amagerian—a blend of the two ways of life. The change represents a special case of acculturation in that the cultural identity became complete, and it is therefore termed amalgamation.

The third phase comprised approximately the first half of the twentieth century, during which time the island was urbanized. Here the dynamics of change constitute a special case of acculturation in that former rural differences were leveled, and rural and urban ways of life became virtually identical. This process is termed assimilation because the product was not a new culture, but a survival of one of the old—the urban—into which the other had been absorbed or assimilated.

The process by which cultures change when in prolonged contact entails the selection of traits from the donor culture, their modification, and the subsequent adjustments made in the host culture. In the case under study, selection and the direction of borrowing varied. In the first phase, the Dutch were wholly exclusive, accepting nothing Danish. The Danish borrowed forms of technology and modes of dress from the Dutch, with a sporadic infusion of other traits. In the second phase, the Danes continued to utilize traits borrowed in phase one, and Dutch festive practices became more widespread. The Dutch adopted the Danish language, which they embellished with a certain tonality that spread back to the Danes. The two halves of the island continued to differ for some time in forms of government and law, since the authority of the national government presented obstacles to adjustment to local circumstances. In the last phase, those traits distinguishing Amager islanders from Copenhageners, specifically occupation, clothing, dialect, government, and legal institutions, as well as forms of celebrating the yearly holidays and rites of passage, were abandoned for city ways.

Traits borrowed in all phases were modified, but the process was remarkable for the superficial nature of this modification, which left the traits substantially the same as in the parent culture. The host culture was necessarily altered with each increment, but only to the extent that it now possessed the borrowed forms of behavior; the process was not marked by chain reactions resulting in extensive and dependent secondary changes nor by basic reorganization of culture patterning and orientation. The minimal adjustive reaction in the host cultures is associated with a near absence of culture conflict and may be traced to the fact that the differences in behavior patterns, great in the eyes of participants and contemporary observers, were actually only variants of a single generalized way of life, the Northwestern European culture. Conflicts between individuals and between communities of the two cultures did occur, but they were social conflicts, not cultural ones. They did not reflect contrasts in life ways, but were economically based rivalries for the right to use the same resources. In contrast to the modification of traits and cultural wholes, selectivity is not understandable primarily in cultural terms. Even though some borrowing, including significant technological accretions, may be regarded as a response to indigenous culturally defined values oriented toward well-being, selectivity as a whole was very responsive to noncultural influences.

A distinction between cultural and social process is implicit in the history of change on Amager island. Cultural process concerns the fate of culture traits and culture wholes in a dynamic situation; social process concerns the formation and maintenance of social groups. On Amager, the successive cultural phases of acculturation, amalgamation, and assimilation were associated with three phases in social alignment: phase one, in which the island was divided into two ethnic societies; phase two, in which the island formed a single folk society; and phase three, in which the island population was incorporated into the large metropolitan agglomeration of Copenhagen. In the creation and maintenance of these social groupings, three phenomena were prominent: intragroup interaction, communication, and group consciousness.

In phase one of this social history, Dutch intragroup interaction was intense and well structured, characterized by a strong communalistic government, an active church, endogamy, and a high degree of economic cooperation. The social life of the Dutch of the whole area focused upon the mother village. For the Danish islanders, social cohesion was relatively weak and was expressed primarily by attendance at a single church and submission to the authority of the king of Denmark, although a network of kinship ties through intermarriage was undoubtedly a salient factor. Within their villages, communal organization was largely imposed by the national government and expressed in the mandatory corvée rather than voluntary communalism. Cooperation between farmers was minimized by the demands of villeinage upon work time. Social relations between the Dutch and the Danish communities were limited to casual encounters in the market and to the granting of loans by the Dutch. Other economic cooperation was absent, and intermarriage was precluded by Dutch endogamy. Means of communication within each ethnic group were efficient, but between the halves were minimal by virtue of the possession of different languages and lack of mutual understanding in the face of contrasts in way of life. Dutch group consciousness was strong. The cultural practices that distinguished them from their neighbors functioned as symbols of their social integrity and economic superiority. The Danes had a relatively weak sense of group consciousness, and opportunistically adopted technological traits, modes of dress, and ritual practices which were patent symbols of the Dutch way of life.

In phase two, intragroup interaction expanded to join the ethnic moieties into a single folk society. Through intermarriage a common kinship network spread over the entire island. Economic cooperation made all Amagerians part of a single agricultural unit. Churches became the meeting places of local residents regardless of ethnic background. Communication within the island was facilitated by the spread of Danish as the common language and by the removal of class distinctions and marriage prohibitions hindering individual social intercourse. The amalgamation of culture eliminated misunderstandings derived from differences in way of life. Group consciousness of the emergent Amagerian folk culture now focused upon the island as a whole, as something distinct from the rest of Denmark. It found symbolic expression in common values resting upon unique shared forms of dress, dialect, architecture, ritual, and agriculture. Technological primitivity in means of land transportation isolated Amagerians from other Danes but it was not a serious impediment to intrainsular communication, and the total effect was to reinforce the unity of the hybrid population, which was epitomized in the reference to themselves as the "Dutch Amagerians" or the "King's Amagerians."

In phase three, interaction between the island and the capital developed rapidly as the Amager population entered the metropolitan labor market, intermarried, and developed ties based upon mutual interests. Communication became rapid and easy as means of transportation were modernized, and was facilitated by the minimization of cultural contrasts by substituting the Copenhagen dialect for that of the island and by dropping unique cultural practices, especially with respect to clothing and ritual. Group consciousness came to be focused upon the capital. Urban modes of dress, speech, and ritual became symbols of belonging to the capital population rather than to a folk enclave.

In the three phases of social change, aggression and hostility were constrained, since overt expression would have represented revolt against national authority in the form of the king and, later, the parliament. Except through sanctioned legal channels, disagreements had no outlet other than grumbling. The small amount of social conflict must be attributed in part to the occurrence of the process in the context of a national government. However, submission to national authority requires that the different peoples concerned be capable of integrating their ways of life, including forms of social organization and evaluation of material goals and punitive strictures. Surely, then, the relatively smooth social transitions were functions of the associated conflict-free cultural changes.

In short, while Amagerian social and cultural processes are analyzable as different phenomena, the three phases of social change were dynamically linked with the three phases of cultural change. This was a reciprocal dependency. In the social process on Amager, intragroup interaction was culturally based, i.e., upon established economic and social institutions. Communication was based upon the function of such culture traits as language, marriage rules, transportation, or even the whole culture regarded as a system of shared understandings. The expression of group consciousness was largely a matter of culture patterns functioning as symbols.

Conversely, social alignments affected culture change in determining the neighboring social groups that bore the cultures and accepted the changes. Beyond this, the process of social change was a factor in the process of cultural change in its influence upon selectivity in borrowing. Insofar as borrowed traits contribute directly to improvement in standard of living, they may be regarded as responding primarily to cultural factors. Some selectivity, however, is best understood in terms of the social process. To take the outstanding examples, language changes in all phases were correlated with the development of new communication areas and with areas unified in group symbols; changes in modes of dress, with practical advantages indicated for the last phase, only, were clearly significant in symbolizing changes in group membership; realignments in the sharing of life-cycle and holiday rituals were also referable to changes in the application of group symbols. In addition, those cultural trait selections responding to cultural factors were also influenced by social ones; changes in forms of agriculture, for example, not only were responses to cultural values but functioned as symbols of the social unity of the Dutch in phase one and of the island as a whole in phase two, just as urban occupations became a symbol of membership in the urban group of phase three.

In the final analysis, therefore, a study of social and cultural dynamics requires one to think in terms of a single sociocultural process. In Amager's history it is found that only minimal cultural or social conflict occurred, and that the sociocultural process was characterized by ease. Had there been cultural conflict resulting from profound differences in way of life, it might be expected that the social changes would have been hampered. Conversely, social conflict could have offered barriers to communication and inter-action which might have hindered the processes of cultural change.

The sociocultural interaction of Dane and Dutchman on Amager island may be termed a case study in acculturation, and we have even somewhat timidly utilized the term to characterize the urbanization of the island. Our findings seem to suggest, however, that culture contact between two offshoots of the same basic tradition results in developments notably dissimilar from those that occur when strikingly different cultures meet. Neither the clash of values nor the difficulties of syncretization are present except as social factors intrude. Whether it is appropriate for such different phenomena to be encompassed by the single term acculturation we leave for the reader to decide. But however named, the processes involved are different.

2: The Community: Dragor

WITHIN Denmark and the island of Amager, attention now focuses upon a single community—Dragor (Dragør). And out of the centuries of changing social life of this community we shall concentrate on only the last phase, that of urban assimilation. To begin this focus and concentration, let us look at the community as a physical entity.

Old Dragor

In the 1890's the straw-roofed buildings hugged tightly against the lookout tower and plank walks of the harbor. Behind them lay open fields, meadow, and park.

A small community of fishermen-agriculturalists inhabited this site off and on throughout the Neolithic, Bronze, and Iron ages. In medieval times, enormous shoals of herring attracted merchants and fishermen of the Hansa League. Abandoned in the cold months, the market place saw as many as 20,000 men in the summers during the twelfth to fifteenth centuries. Then came years at a stretch when the herring did not appear, and with the disappearance of the fish went the men. Sixteenth- and seventeenth-century visitors found only a tiny hamlet of decrepit cottages inhabited by poor fishermen and their families. Records of former greatness collected dust in the archives of the disbanded Hansa cities.

Early in the eighteenth century the hamlet began to grow again. The little harbor was deep and attracted the younger sons of neighboring well-to-do farmers, who bought ships and engaged in maritime trade. By 1784 Dragor was the second largest shipping center in the entire kingdom, with 130 ships registered and

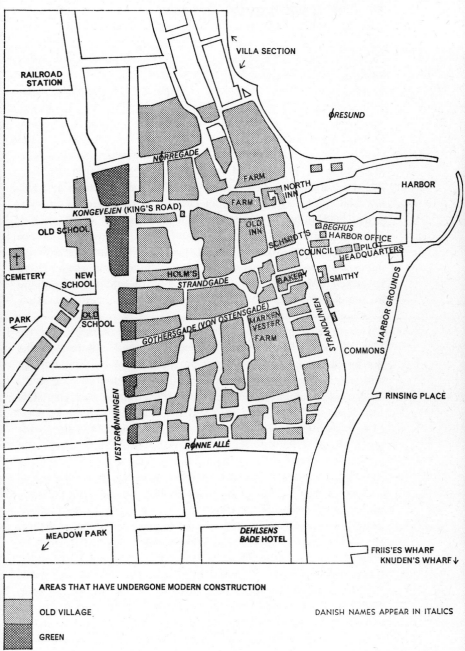

DRAGOR *(DRAGØR)* 1957

AREAS THAT HAVE UNDERGONE MODERN CONSTRUCTION

OLD VILLAGE

GREEN

DANISH NAMES APPEAR IN ITALICS

a population of about 1,250. At this peak the town was prosperous and busy. Subsequent decades witnessed a barely percep-
tible yet steady deterioration. By 1877 the harbor dropped to
third largest shipping center with seventy-eight ships and 1,850
people. The number of registered ships fell off regularly, especially during the last years of the century, while the population
stabilized at approximately 1900 inhabitants. In the year 1900,
the harbor of Dragor sheltered only ten ships.

The period 1890–1900 is our ethnographic baseline—the
touchstone for the study of twentieth century developments. It is
the last decade of a two-century period of prosperous island and
international sailing. Subsequent decades were to see social, economic, and cultural orientations turn inland to the city.

But to return to nineteenth-century Dragor, it was a maze of
narrow, crooked streets, closely packed with small dwellings.
Along the beach at the south end was a communal meadow. There
fishermen dried their nets, domestic animals and fowl wandered
in search of food, block-long lengths of raw linen were sun-
bleached, and women spread clothes out to dry.

Dragor was approached from Copenhagen to the north by "the
king's road" (*Kongevejen*). Where this road approached the
northwest corner of the village it passed the new red-brick church
and school buildings. Entering the village, it detoured around the
swine yard and barn of one of the three farms, went by "Old
Inn" (*Gammel Kro*) and ended at the harbor, the focus of local
life. There one saw the council house (*raadhuset*), the headquarters and lookout tower of the Royal Sound Pilots, the "North
Inn" (*Nordre Kro*), the smithy, and a general store.

The perception of a town includes smelling and listening as
well as seeing. Typical of its time, Dragor was far less attractive
to the nose than to the eyes. Sanitary facilities were minimal.
Sewage disposal was no more than the medieval open or board-
covered drainage ditch in the road, cleaned more frequently by
the rooting of the pigs than by the four village watchmen or by
householders. Night soil was deposited on one of the half dozen
middens located at strategic places in the town. In fall and early
winter winds brought in the disagreeable odor of tons of rotting
seaweed from the beach and the harbor, while within the village
three farms contributed their share from poorly drained stalls,
pig sties, and manure piles.

To these odors must be added the more comfortable, even pleasant ones. Heating and cooking, done with wood or coal fires, laid a pall of smoke on a cold winter eve. Around about the house the wet straw roof, the beer-brewing pot, the barrel of salted herring, the cooking cabbage—all contributed to the local fragrance.

To the romantic ear, the town was enchanting. Every hour during the night a watchman could be heard, his little song badly sung, but loud, an assurance that all was well, that for the moment at least no fire rushed along the straw roofs, no gale threatened boats and nets, no hijackers attacked the cargoes in the harbor. In the morning hours the shouts of wagon men were heard urging their horses forward toward Copenhagen, horse hooves clattering now loudly on cobblestone, now softly on hard-packed dirt. At the harbor the clang of metal against metal was a steady reminder that the smith was at his job, although generally not too busy to watch the freighters when shouted orders, chanted heave ho's, and flapping sails announced the departure or arrival of ship and crew. Small fishing boats, silent as they left, were greeted on return with loud-shouted conversation as each wanted to know what catch the other had made. Morning and night, cows bellowed and shuffled as they made their way through the town. Here and there geese honked raucously as they rushed for a handout of scraps, or guided a lost member through the narrow streets back to the flock. Equally irregular, but much more exciting, was the hornblower, whose march through the streets announced that a ship was stranded. And all the while, the church bells chimed the hours—and the days, and the years, and the centuries.

This was a little world. Houses, rooms, streets, boats, ships, and carriages—all were small and cramped. But this was a little world in another sense too, for Dragorians were isolated and conservative, keeping closely to their village, meeting at times people from other parts of the island and from other fishing villages, but strangers to the life of the city dweller. Trips to Copenhagen, whether by land or by sea, were rare. When they did occur the Dragorian rarely ventured beyond the market place, where he met other Dragorians or Amagerians rather than Copenhageners. The town was a busy seaport and fishing center, but intercourse with outsiders was remarkably limited, other than with men from small neighboring fishing villages on the Sound.

The ships' crews that stopped off were local people from locally owned ships sailing under local skippers, and so-called "foreign" fishermen were familiar as regular seasonal visitors from nearby harbors. Sailors visited strange and distant ports seeing exotic things, yet the sailor spent most of his time on the wooden ships with his fellow Danes and Dragorians, and came home little changed for so much travel, richer primarily by the possession of a French shawl or a Chinese vase. Older women still wore a costume unique to them, identifying them as belonging to the village, and Dragorian speech, too, betrayed a provinciality, for rather than the language of the capital one heard a dialect of Scandian, the tongue once common in the Danish and Swedish towns surrounding the Sound, with a Dutch tonality added by the many immigrants of the preceding centuries from Store Magleby.

Isolated by primitive and expensive methods of communication as well as by restricted local interests, Dragorians had a small-community mentality that knew little beyond Dragor, Amager, and the Sound. A visitor from beyond this familiar world sent women and children scurrying for shelter to peek gingerly, from the safety of a hiding place, at the strange invader. More than once a Copenhagener occasioned an excited child to shout, "Mother, mother, I saw a foreigner!"

Modern Dragor

The census figures for Dragor increased but slightly during the early decades of the twentieth century. In 1890 there were 1,945 people, the figure dropping to about 1,850 in 1900, but then advancing gradually, reaching 2,093 in 1940. Approximately 1,000 people arrived in the 1940's with the construction of apartment houses and multiple-dwelling units in the southern part of the settlement, and by 1955 there were 3,500 residents within the corporate limits. The change expressed here in numbers was but one of many dramatic changes experienced by Dragorians in the new century.

Immigrants from Copenhagen accounted for the growth of the community. At the turn of the century the first Copenhageners came as summer residents. They built small villas in the northern end of the village which were left uninhabited during the greater part of the year (and as a result they are not represented in the census figures). In 1907 a railroad was built between the capital and Dragor. Although railroad travel was not cheap, it was reasonable enough for people in the professional classes and it was fast. Thus it became feasible for the villa people to remodel their houses and live all year round in this beautiful little harbor town. The real expansion waited, however, until after World War II.

By that time the need for housing was acute in the capital since the population there had skyrocketed during the war years when it had been impossible to build residences. It was practical to meet this need by the construction of suburban communities because of the developments that had taken place in the area of communication and transportation. Starting in the nineties and accelerating rapidly in the twentieth century, people had taken to bicycles, which made them a great deal more ambulatory than ever before. Youngsters and aged alike took to wheels; cripples had custom-built models (often tricycles), while infants and small children were accommodated in special seats on the front or the back of the bicycle, or on both the front and the back. In addition, however, the bus, which replaced the train, provided regular, dependable transportation at rates reasonable enough for the average commuting laborer or white-collar worker. The postwar years in Denmark also witnessed a large increase in the number of motorized bicycles and scooters, an increase which reached startling velocity between 1950 and 1955. Automobiles, on the other hand, remain a luxury enjoyed by few and are of significance for daily communication primarily for the professional classes, the villa people.

A villa quarter now stretches northward along the waterfront where deep lots with large lawns and flower gardens provide an attractive setting for the houses of the well-to-do. To the south is "Meadow Park," a moderately priced housing development of apartment houses and one-family dwellings. The town looks quite different from the nineties; and yet, not so much. Its heart is still "Old Town" and the harbor. The medieval drainage ditches have disappeared, but the houses and street plan are the same, and the community savors an essence of antiquity.

3: Dragor as a Man's World

Dragorian Men of Old

DRAGOR was a harbor town and the sea touched the life of its every inhabitant. The majority of the men sailed in the merchant marine or fished in local waters, and shipboard life was so highly valued that to have any other occupation was embarrassing. Few men working ashore were free of a compulsion to describe the physical incapacity or forced filial promise that explained or rationalized their lesser-esteemed position.

Merchant Sailing

Eight tenths of the men were mariners, and of these approximately ninety were skippers, ships' officers, or pilots who had been able to afford the requisite navigational training because their fathers before them had been equally well placed. Membership in one of these well-to-do families was also the best promise of a ship to command and attainment of the acme of these highly regarded titles, that of shipmaster (*skibsfører*) or *skipper*.

But a shipmaster could rarely succeed on family help alone.

The typical Dragorian skipper of the nineties was an entrepreneur. The driving power of his vessel came from sails, and whether small and used for insular trade or large enough to sail to other continents, his ship was his business. Using his cabin as an office he contracted to carry Amager cabbages to the provinces, a load of wood from Sweden to Denmark, or bananas from the Canary Islands to Europe. Rarely did he know where he would sail from his next destination, and his skill in seamanship had to be matched by his ability to find a cargo. The ship and its captain, then, were a business enterprise, a combination of capital and skill, and in the successful enterprise the captain was well paid.

To the observer it would seem that ownership of a ship was a vital necessity if sufficient initiative were to be maintained and, indeed, it so happens that most shipmasters were also owners or part owners of their vessels. For two centuries Dragor had been the home port of a large number of sailing ships, at times the second or third largest harbor of registration in all of Denmark. It is therefore hardly surprising to find that the majority of the sea captains had obtained ships by birth or marriage, those not inheriting from a father or grandfather often having married a shipowner's daughter. At the same time, when large families were the rule, the man who became too old to sail or who had acquired more than one ship, need rarely hire a captain, for it was far better business to put the vessel in the hands of a relative who would not be lacking in the necessary initiative.

Approximately 150 men were seamen. Most of the crews of Dragorian skippers were composed of these local men, and to them went the manual labor of managing sails and lines as well as such specialized jobs as ship's cook, ship's carpenter, or coxswain.

In the nineties, most sailing in northern waters was still done in smaller craft which could not navigate in the ice-bound winter. Between December and April they turned the harbor into a moored jungle of masts and rigging, the sign that the men of the sea were at home.

Piloting

The enforced inactivity of midwinter was common to all of the men who sailed, including pilots. In still other respects the life of the pilot was similar to that of the skipper, a similarity, however, which fell considerably short of an identity. Thus, the pilot commanded a ship, but only through the dangerous Sound and no more; he also had a good income, but not as much as the more successful skippers and without the latter's virtually unlimited earning potential, as illustrated by Maersk Lines, built up by multimillionaire A. P. Møller from the ship of his grandfather, a Dragorian skipper, and the Isbrandtsen Lines of the United States, founded by Møller's Dragorian cousin Hans Isbrandtsen. Finally, the pilot often was absent from his family, although never for such long, unbroken lengths of time.

The job of the pilot was to meet ships coming from the Baltic or the Kattegat and to guide them through the narrow channel of the Sound to the port of Copenhagen or Elsinore. Prolonged periods when no ships came were followed by the sudden arrival of perhaps hundreds when the wind suddenly picked up or changed, each requiring the immediate services of a channel pilot. At such a time every man would be on duty, in addition to which much illegal piloting was done by other villagers. When the traffic was less, some of the staff could stay in their homes, subject to call when their turn came.

At the Royal Pilot Station was a board on which was painted the name of each man, followed by a letter indicating whether the man was on duty, at home, or ill. When on duty, the pilot cruised back and forth in the pilot boat, specially marked with a large red stripe on the sail, spending nights and quiet hours on board the lighthouse ship in Drogden Bay. Waiting hours on the lighthouse ship were spent at cards, reading, hobbies such as carving model ships or painting, or perhaps practical tasks which might include repairing the family's leather-topped wooden shoes. These activities contrasted with the action-charged moment when the small pilot boat approached the side of a ship to allow the pilot to perform his task, for climbing up a free-hanging rope ladder, a tricky task at best, was all the more so and dangerous to boot when the seas were high. The trip to Copenhagen or Elsinore normally lasted only a few hours, but could stretch into days if the vessel were becalmed. Port reached, the pilot went to an inn to meet or wait for others until there were enough collected to fill a hired coach to carry them back to the village. The waiting period was made easier by a glass of beer, a shot of *aquavitæ,* or a rum toddy, and not infrequently the worst occupational hazard proved to be alcoholism.

The amount of work depended on the traffic, and so did the pay. The yearly income of the pilot station, minus 4 per cent for widows, and 6 per cent for upkeep of the boats, was divided into man-parts. Senior pilots got a full part, junior pilots, that is, those with only a few years of experience, three fourths of a part, reserve pilots, who were called only when the others were all busy, one fourth. Highest paid were the inspector and the book-keeper, each getting, respectively, two parts and one and a half parts.

Fishing

Approximately one hundred men were full-time fishermen. The sea sporadically deprived the great majority of Dragorian families of the presence of their adult men. In fishing, however, family life was also influenced by the involvement of the wife and children in the enterprise. All members of the domestic family gave regular assistance to the family head in cleaning, repairing, and constructing equipment. A son, even as a child, was commonly a sailing assistant, and many a woman peddled her husband's fish in Dragor or neighboring villages. A few fisher wives took the early morning carriage to "Old Beach" (*Gammelstrand*), the famous fish market in Copenhagen, where they joined others of their kind from Taarbæk, Skovshoved, and other nearby harbors to sell their product to city housewives.

Eel was the main summer fish and cod the winter one, with herring, shrimp, mackerel, gar pike, and flounder of much lesser importance.

As a favorite food of the Danes, eel commanded a good price and was important to Dragorian fishermen because it appeared in commercial quantities every summer, the season lasting from the first of April until September, October, or November. Lines totaling up to 2,000 hooks were set for them as well as traps, the latter used mainly in August and September when full-grown eel (*blankaal*) visited the shallow waters of the coast on dark, moonless, east-wind nights.

Traps were expensive, and made in various sizes, for they had to just be able to reach from water's bottom to surface. Each fisherman set out two to ten traps, either singly, or one behind the other, the traps always running from the beach into the Sound at a right angle to the shoreline. Each man had his trapping places, and his right to use them was not challenged as long as he continued to utilize them. If unused, however, they were considered available to the firstcomer. Each such trapping place had a name and a reputation, "the flat stone" (*den flade sten*) and "the three stones" (*de tre stene*), for example, being average places, "the speculator" (*spekulanten*) being the most distant from the harbor and taking considerable time to reach, while "the gold set" (*guldsætten*) was known for unusually good catches.

Hooks were set in deeper waters and took a two-man crew.

The fishermen left port at six or seven P.M. and it took two or three hours to sail to the fishing place where the line of baited hooks was fed into the water from trays. The men were then free to sleep in the boat until around one A.M., when the lines were hauled in and the fish thrown into a standing barrel of water. By five-thirty or six in the morning, the fishermen were home again in time to send the catch on to Copenhagen.

Two other methods of eel fishing should be mentioned, although they were only sporadically employed. Using one method, the fishermen poled a small flat-bottomed boat over the shallow eel waters in the daytime, or at night using an oil lamp to illuminate, and impaled the frightened prey with a barbed or saw-toothed (respectively, *piglyster* or *savlyster*) lyster.

The other method, used mostly by old men or women during summer days in water shallow enough for wading, involved two persons working as a team. One held a wooden-framed, net-covered scoop into which the eel were chased by thrusting the undergrowth with a kind of toothless wooden rake. The person with the scoop held his bare toe against the net to feel the prize; he then scooped it up and placed it in a floating barrel half full of water.

Cod showed up in marketable amounts in eel traps and on the lines, but were primarily a winter fish, their season lasting from October to April. According to a widespread Danish belief, one should preferably not eat cod "when there is no *r* in the [name of the] month," which is to say not in the summer, because in the winter season the fish is not only much fatter and tastier but is better preserved by the cold. They were taken for the most part with traps, which were the same as those used for eel and shrimp except larger in diameter and mesh, but were also caught on the same lines used for eel fishing. To get them with hook, however, required setting the lines in the deep waters, and only a couple of the largest boats could go that far and still have time to set and haul in the lines.

In most years ice was too heavy and storms too severe to permit profitable fishing between late December and March. A poor man, fisherman or not, could not, however, value his time very highly, and frequently tried his hand at difficult, poorly rewarded ice fishing. Chopping a hole through the ice with an ax, he jigged (*pilkede*) for cod, using a shiny piece of herring-shaped metal into which two large hooks were fused. Attached to a line long enough to reach the bottom of the Sound, the hook was pulled upward, its movements attracting the cod which came close enough to be hooked, as often in the tail or stomach as in the mouth. Closer to the beach one might see men chopping holes in the ice and poking rapidly up and down in the greenery on the bottom with a lyster until the blind stabbing produced an eel. Although these two methods did not pay well, the equipment was cheap, the technique required very little skill, and there were few conflicting demands upon a person's time in that part of the year.

Salvaging

Fishing trips and work on equipment were dropped once or twice a month when the town crier's (*bytjeners*) horn, blowing in *gader* and *stræder,* announced that a ship had run aground in the Sound. Within the hour the first group of available men was crowded into the town dinghy and headed for the distressed craft. There the mayor (*foged*), a retired sea captain, climbed aboard the grounded ship, accompanied by his fellow citizens, to present a contract establishing the terms of the salvage job. A number of fishermen sailed out in their own boats, several boats in addition to that of the town being necessary to remove the cargo, for it was seldom that a ship could be saved without lightening its load. The local crew was joined by professional salvagers from Svitzer's Salvage Enterprise of Copenhagen, which had some years before entered into contract with the town, since the latter did not have the specialized equipment and skills necessary for salvaging large, iron-hulled ships. Working generally for several days, the men moved the contents of the ship's holds to the small boats to be ferried ashore. In most cases the lightened ship could eventually be floated free of the shallow bank which imprisoned it, otherwise as much of it as was possible was also salvaged.

The division of the profits, as documented for the year 1887, gave 50 per cent to Svitzer's and 50 per cent to the town and its inhabitants, the latter half divided as follows:

Municipal officials: mayor 3 per cent; four
    representatives, ¼ per cent each . . . . 4 per cent
Municipal treasuries: town treasury, 4 per cent;
    harbor treasury, 9 per cent; school treasury,

3 per cent............................16 per cent
Widows: to each of sixty, 33 *øre* for each
  2000 *kroner*............................variable
Unspecified expenses....................4 to 5 per cent
Men and Boats: ⅓ to the boats; ⅔ to the
  men............................about 75 per cent

Only men and boat owners whose domicile was in Dragor could participate, since the town had a monopoly on salvage operations in that part of the Sound. The boat owners were paid according to the number of loads carried. The men were paid by man-parts (*mandparter*). Every man over eighteen years of age who made his living on the seas got a full man-part. Sea people between ages sixteen and eighteen and men who did not work at sea were entitled to one half a man-part, while nonseamen between sixteen and eighteen years got only one fourth a part. Those men who had registered as sick retained the man-part to which they would be entitled if they had worked. Old men no longer able to participate got a half part. The mayor and town representatives each got two man-parts in addition to their regular percentage of the total, and school teachers and other town functionaries received one, one and one-half, or two parts.

Dragorians also earned some money on small, private salvage jobs, of which one half of the earnings went to the town treasury. Salvaging was thus extremely important to the town's economy, spreading a money income widely within its confines and providing sufficient municipal income to free all citizens from payment of communal taxes of any kind.

In their eagerness to profit from the misfortune of stranded ships Dragorians might at times use somewhat unethical tactics, although they were never accused of deliberately changing channel markers to cause groundings, as is known to have occurred in other parts of the world. Thus, there is the story, perhaps apocryphal, that when a large ship went aground in the late 1880's and was approached by the town's boat it was noticed that the ship's sails were being hoisted in an attempt to move off the sandbank. The Dragorians shouted to the captain to furl his sails if he did not want to wreck his ship. The captain promptly obeyed and soon found himself signing a salvage contract. But no sooner was he committed to pay for help than he heard the command given to raise his sails, which, when done, sufficed to free the ship.

Farming

The village had a rustic appearance because of the presence of three farms in or near its center. These buildings, following Danish practice, had dwelling and barn under a single roof and were oriented around a rectangular courtyard. Local agricultural activities differed from those of Denmark beyond Amager in the regional specialization on vegetable cultivation for the Copenhagen market. Produce included onions, leeks, red and white cabbage, cauliflower, kale, carrots, celery, potatoes, and thyme, with only a bit of grain, the latter mostly barley.

All three of the farmers were wealthy by local standards, but their participation in communal life was limited to the extent that their occupational interests were shared with the Dutch-descended Store Magleby farmers, to whom two of them were related. They paid land taxes to "Dutchtown" (*Hollænderbyen*), as Store Magleby was locally called, cooperated with Dutch farmers in the exchange of services and equipment, and took part in their festivities. These considerations aside, the farmers were like their fellow Dragorians in one way at least. They were relatively inactive in the winter months, citing the adage that the plow must be stored in the barn by Christmas to assure a good harvest the following season.

Bleaching

In warmer months, ten families of bleachers covered the village meadows with large lengths of linen. Husband and wife formed a team in the processing of these goods, which were consigned to them for treatment by Copenhagen merchants. The woman boiled the cloth in large iron caldrons three feet deep and four feet wide at the top. The man and his sons carted the boiled linen to the beach where it was hand-rinsed in the Sound and picketed on the grass to sun-bleach. A summer occupation, lasting from the last of April until some time in September, it provided enough money to support the family modestly for the whole year.

Service Occupations

In the year 1890 the village counted twenty-nine shopkeepers, forty craftsmen, six drayers and four innkeepers as well as a priest and four school teachers. The number of shopkeepers is proportionately large, but most of them were old people using a single room, or even just a chest in the bedroom, as a place to do business with a microscopic inventory. For example, one old seaman used a room in his house near the harbor as a sales place for fats and butter, the latter being wrapped in old newspapers so that one "could read the butter" when the wrapping was removed. A number of retired seamen used saved earnings to start small grocery stores in their homes and old women often dealt in home-made sugar candy, needles and thread, or other household items. Although some shops had substantial business, most were so small that they interfered only intermittently with housekeeping and other sedentary duties.

Craftsmen were of two kinds, those such as the blacksmith and shipbuilders directly supported by the local sailing fleet, and others such as carpenters and masons supplying the needs of the populace. In the winter, neither kind of craft offered very much employment. In addition to stoppages brought about by inclement weather, the inactivity of the men of the sea brought all trade to a minimum, for unemployed men were not inclined to engage help if it could be avoided.

The barber warrants special mention. Since most men shaved themselves and had their hair cut by their wives, it was only occasionally that he was asked to call at a house to practice his specialty. His living was gained by an aspect of his occupation that has since ceased to be associated with the trade, the pulling of teeth and bloodletting. His business did not require a shop and his steadiest income came from his service as manager (*økonom*) of the village poorhouse. In addition to the barber an experience-trained midwife was in residence. Other medical services were nonexistent until the end of the decade when a physician started calling at the village once a week.

Modern Men

Each male occupation of the last century has changed, and each is a worthy subject of analysis. But in terms of communal life, these specific changes are of minor importance, for relatively few men are now engaged in the old primary occupations. Forty fishermen, six pilots, a scattering of seamen sailing nonlocal ships, and three farmers are all that remain in a population now num-

bering 3,500. Shopkeepers, certain craftsmen, and draymen survived, of course, but their orientations are to the new way of life.
And this new way of life is enmeshed in the modern industrial-
commercial economy of Copenhagen and its suburbs.

The modern Dragorian normally works outside the community
in a factory, office, or shop that requires his regular presence on
weekdays and Saturday mornings. Typically he is not his own
boss, although some "bosses" live in the villa section of the
modern community. His work may or may not challenge him,
but in any case he has evenings and weekends when he can pursue
hobbies and sports. The predictable result has been a growing
emphasis on leisure-time activities.

The annual cycle too has changed. The long quiet winter, that
formerly gave every man a change of pace, is now replaced by
regular, and short, winter and summer vacations. With all of these
changes has gone the intimate communality of Dragorian men.
No longer do they congregate at the harbor in the evenings, or
exchange visits in the winter. The sea has ceased to bind them
in a shared maritime interest. Each goes his own way. The dis-
persion into the urban network of work-a-day jobs reflects itself
in the community as a concentration of each individual on his
own home and his own private circle of friends.

How did this great change come about?

By the turn of the century, Dragor's local economy was tail-
spinning in the face of technological progress. The fishermen
adapted well enough to mechanical change. By 1905 Dragorian
fishermen were devoting much of their conversation to the qualities and advantages of the newly available motors. All had some
knowledge of the mechanics of steam and internal-combustion
engines, but the significance of these developments for their own
work largely escaped them, and the majority were not at once
disposed to make the necessary adjustments for what they considered debatable advantages. Not the least of the considerations
was cost—for motorized boats were larger and motors themselves
very expensive. By 1906, however, two of the fishermen had
motorized boats, and their example gave courage to others who
had theirs by 1908. After that, the advantage of motors was no
longer argued, and conversion from sail was primarily a question
of financing. Within a decade sail boats were completely obsolete.
Those who did not have new boats sought work in partnership

with those who did. Adaptations of the essentially unchanged fishing procedures were readily made.

Organizationally, an association was established. In 1904, a meeting of all the fishermen was held to form the Dragor Fishing Association (*Dragør Fiskeriforening*) patterned on associations of other parts of Denmark. A council (*bestyrelse*) of five men was elected, one of whom was designated foreman and another treasurer. These men then drew up a set of rules for the running of the society, based on the will of the fishermen as expressed by a majority vote in a meeting held the following January. Such a meeting was scheduled annually thereafter. The association is still active. Each year half of the officers are elected, but in practice incumbents are generally re-elected so that the turnover is very slow.

The reasons for founding the society, and its aims, were, in part, to provide for regular transportation of fish to the market in Copenhagen at a saving to members, who otherwise had to make individual arrangements. This was arranged through a local draying company. It was also planned to persuade the town council to reserve a special section of the harbor for the exclusive use of Dragorian fishermen who were being crowded out by non-Dragorian boats, as well as by the pleasure craft that came more and more into evidence as leisure sailing flourished. They now have their own berths, permanently assigned. The association intended as well to negotiate to keep fish prices up, but in this has never known consistent success.

The union with other fishermen into a more comprehensive society was also envisaged, and was accomplished in 1909 when they joined with other towns of the Sound area of Denmark to form the Sound's Cooperative Fishing Association (*Sundet Samvirkende Fiskeriforeningen*). The purpose of this larger association was to provide a set of rules applicable for all Sound fishing, a proposal of special interest to Dragorians who had lost much of their standing equipment to trawlers. According to national law, fishermen of certain areas have the right to regulate fishing practices by majority vote, subject to the approval of the central government. By the efforts of the cooperative association, it was possible to prohibit the trawling which menaced local equipment.

All of the fishermen in Dragor belong to the association. According to association rules, a man must derive at least three fifths of his income from fishing in order to vote, so that only forty members currently have voting privileges. Universal membership is assured by the advantages accruing exclusively to members: first, the net-drying places are rented from the community by the association and are at the disposal of members. Although, under national law, fishermen are indiscriminately allowed the rental of community property for net drying, it proves easier for the Dragorian to work through the society than to make his own arrangements. Second, the society owns a large stove and vat for use in the treatment of nets. Third, the association, in conjunction with the more recently formed Sport Sailing Club (*Sejlsportsklubben*), owns and maintains equipment (a motorized unit replacing a hand winch in 1953) for hauling boats on land for winter layovers and for repairs.

All fishing societies in Denmark, except those of southern Jutland, are united into the Danish Fishing Association (*Dansk Fiskeriforening*), made up of 175 local societies. Expenditures are met by the local societies out of members' yearly dues. This association publishes a monthly newspaper, the *Dansk Fiskeritidende,* featuring information pertinent to the practical problems of the fishermen as well as data on legislation which may affect their interests. The society also provides the advantage of acting as intermediary to central government authorities for the common benefit of all fishermen.

In spite of adaptability and organization, broader developments were beyond the control of local fishermen. With modern methods of transportation, fish from more distant areas can now be marketed in Copenhagen at costs under those for Dragorian fish. In recent decades, the bottom has dropped out of local fishing. It is moribund.

The shipowners reacted less effectively to purely technological change. The Dragor Ship Owners and Shipmasters Society (*Dragør Skibsreder og Skibsfører Forening*), founded in the 1870's to unite its members for mutual benefit, and commonly known as the "Skippers' Society" (*Skipperforeningen*), served for little more than pleasure and debate in the process of change. Only a couple of local men had the business acumen and capital necessary to finance steel-hulled, steam-driven vessels. Only a few were willing to commit the village to the expense of deepening the harbor to accommodate the new craft. Many apparently did not realize the rapidity with which sailing craft would become obsolete, and invested in old sailing ships, by then a glut on the market. In any case, by World War I, the merchant marine lost its importance for the community as large-scale operations in other ports emerged into prominence.

The pilot station too became relatively insignificant on the local scene. As a result of improved methods of channel marking, small ships no longer needed piloting. Large ships, independent of the weather, did not need to queue up to descend en masse when the wind picked up. Thus there was no longer a need for large reserve numbers of pilots. The number of pilots decreased from seventeen in 1906 to an average of eight during the period between the two world wars. There have been no more than six at any one time since the Second World War. The unofficial, illegal piloting by unlicensed Dragorians has been unreported for more than thirty years.

Salvage has fallen off considerably in the last fifty years. But despite its consistent decline in the face of modern navigational techniques there are still several strandings a year, particularly in winter. The organization of such work, however, has changed significantly. In 1910 the village government was changed to that prescribed by the national government for small communities. By this act Dragor was deprived of its special form of government, financed largely by the profits of salvage operations, and at the same time was deprived of its special concession for the salvaging of ships stranded in its vicinity. Salvaging, instead, was exclusively relegated by the national government to Svitzer Company which had formerly acted solely in a cooperating capacity under Dragorian control. The company, however, found it convenient to continue to draw man power at the old source, particularly for the large crews promptly necessary at those unpredictable moments when wrecks occur. Within Dragor, the men who formerly partook in this work by virtue of their residence formed a society (*bjærgelav*), with a council headed by a foreman and a set of operating rules. Outside of their own full-time specialists, Svitzer Company hires exclusively from this society for assistance in salvage operations within the area. Members, all residents of Dragor, must be available at all hours. This, in effect, limits the group to local fishermen who are alone in the position to answer a call. When a stranding is announced, by telephone or personal message, all members call the foreman and place themselves at his disposal. Not all are employed at once. Crews are rotated, but the entire membership shares equally in the society's remuneration for each operation. Although a meeting is held annually at which officers are elected, the foreman is the only person with real responsibility and he is commonly re-elected. He is chiefly occupied with bookkeeping and the payroll, and for these assignments he is allotted an extra share of the profits.

Although salvage is no longer important to the town as a whole, it represents an important source of income for the remaining fishermen, particularly during the winter months when they are otherwise occupied almost solely with preparations for the coming season.

In various ways, then, the village's marine-oriented economy was thoroughly scuttled, and a centuries-old union of the community culture with the sea ended. The technical progress that brought economic crisis to the village, however, also provided its resolution. Buses, bicycles, private motorized vehicles, and the railway permitted the arrival of Copenhageners in search of homes beyond the burgeoning city. At the same time, these modern forms of transportation permitted Dragorians to commute. As the old forms of local occupation became unprofitable, the villagers turned from the sea to the city for a means of earning a living. In the course of two decades, Dragor found itself a suburb of Copenhagen, with its economic base in Denmark's capital city.

The critical change, in short, was not the mechanization of maritime pursuits, but this process of supplanting old occupations by new. In this, the difficulties of individual adjustment never became a public problem. Those who could or would not change, especially older people, simply continued to follow traditional paths. A small number have managed to this day to enjoy financial as well as social success as pilots or fishermen, and several latter-day skippers successfully transferred to nonlocal commands.

For the rest, the men found jobs without difficulty in the expanding labor market of the region, and their sons are trained and oriented for the land. Among the indigenes as well as among adopted sons, a deep nostalgia for the sea persists. But there is no nostalgia for the poverty and distress of those declining years, and in this seaside location, every man can be a sea captain on weekends.

4: A Woman's Work

THE Danish housewife has been liberated, if one is to believe modern newspaper and magazine advertisements, from much of the drudgery of her calling. Doubtless, housekeeping tasks have been modernized and simplified. Wooden table and white wooden floors were scrubbed in the nineties with brushes and old rags in water fetched from the pump or the storage barrel and heated over the wood stove. In the summer, rugs, bedding, and clothes were taken outside to be beaten in the air.

Washing clothes was a big job done four or five times a year in the warm months. For a day or more before a wash, large tubs were filled with soiled clothes left to soak in water softened by the addition of soda. When the time came, the clothes were put in a large metal caldron and boiled in soapy water over a wood fire. While one batch was boiling the previous batch was scrubbed on a rippled board, after which it was carried to the "rinsing place," a plank platform reaching out over the Sound, where paddle and Sound water finished the job. After drying in the wind or on the grass, most things were simply folded. Bed linen, table cloths, and towels while still slightly damp were rolled, done by folding them lengthwise to a width of no more than two feet, wrapping them on a round stick (about two inches in diameter), and then applying pressure to the linen by rolling it on a flat surface under a flat board some two and a half feet long. The latter, as well as the paddle used to beat the clothes when rinsing, often bore beautifully carved motifs brightly painted. A few fine things, including the man's collarless dress shirt, might be pressed with a heavy iron heated over the kitchen cookstove.

In modern Dragor, these tasks are lightened by vacuum cleaner, electric washing machine, and modern detergents. Other jobs, such as beer brewing, butter churning, cheese making, candle dipping, and especially weaving, are simply no longer on the workday agenda.

Has the housewife's work thereby been significantly lightened?

Hardly! For the community has followed the rest of the Western world in raising its level of aspirations. Look first at one major part of a woman's work—cleaning. While cleaning tasks were formerly more arduous, the standards of cleanliness were considerably lower.

Floor cleaning took time, but the fastidious housekeeper only swept her floors weekly, and probably the majority left at least some of their floor space untouched for far longer periods.

A certain amount of dirt was normal and unnoticed. At least one old lady led her flock of geese daily through her front room to the room where they were kept, and others were known to allow geese regularly in the house. Keeping animals in the house is an ancient European practice, and hardly sets our villagers off from their contemporaries elsewhere. A sixteenth-century German traveler to the Scandian region noted,

And as for young animals, ignoring the presence of dog, cat, chickens, and pigeons which do not matter very much, they have in the house calves, lambs, kids, and piglets. These sleep in the middle of the room during the night, and lick one's face while one is asleep. Thus both man and beast are to be found in the same room, and you can readily imagine what a heavenly fragrance there must be, since there is no place for the odor to escape.[1]

Thus, nineteenth-century standards were relatively high in prohibiting larger animals from entering the house, and modern proscriptions exclude all but pets.

Nor was dusting a daily or regular chore. No one was disturbed that shelves and shelved items collected dust, and one simply developed as part of the normal gesture of picking up an object, the wiping of it with a corner of one's ever-present apron.

As already indicated, washing clothes was a difficult task, but only infrequently performed. The heavy, dark-colored clothes of

[1] Quoted in Axel Steensberg, "Bondens Hverdag," in *Den Danske Bonde, Kulturbilleder,* ed. M. P. Ejerslev (Copenhagen: Nordisk Specialforlag, 1945), p. 101. Authors' translation.

the period were normally worn for protracted periods of time without washing, and table linen was used only for holidays. Even a man's Sunday shirt would do for numerous wearings, with more frequent changing of cuffs and collars.

The twentieth-century Dragorian housewife is now extremely conscientious about cleanliness. Clothes are washed weekly, some daily. Dusting, sweeping, and vacuuming are daily and weekly tasks. The norm, which is often attained, is that floors, shelves, and furniture should be able to pass a white-glove inspection any time of the day, week, or month.

Cooking is another part of a woman's work, and a similar story of change is recounted. A wooden stove was hard to fire up and regulate. But the diet was simple and monotonous. A hot meal was served once a day at noon. The main dish was most often boiled potatoes with a thick brown gravy. Not much effort in that. Just as often, dishes were prepared which, once done, lasted for several days in a row with only reheating required. Examples of the latter would include split-pea soup (*guleærtersuppe*), browned cabbage (*brunkaal*), buttermilk soup (*kærnemælksuppe*), or beer soup (*ølebrød*). Even well-off housewives served economical and easily prepared meals of oatmeal porridge or boiled fish. Other meals, which usually included two breakfasts, an afternoon snack, and a light evening meal in addition to the noon meal, consisted simply of porridge or open-faced sandwiches.

The modern wife and mother may have a gas or electric stove, hot and cold running water, a refrigerator, and prepared purchased foods, but on the whole her cooking chores are probably greatly more time-consuming than were those of her grandmother of the last century. Meals have been reduced from five to three in number, but variety is expected. Breakfast remains a simple meal, with hot or cold cereals, coffee and rolls. But the lunch carried to work or school is typically a well-balanced collection of the now-famous open-faced sandwiches, balanced with fruit and cake. The hot meal not only has shifted to the evening hour but aspires, with varying success, to tasty originality. Although potatoes and gravy are still basic, with occasional reliance on the traditional soups and stews, they are sometimes spelled off with more novel concoctions derived from the far corners of the earth as well as from local inventiveness, and are in any case rounded out with ample use of fish, meat, salads, desserts, and so on. In short, the modernized kitchen is a symbol of more, not less, cooking effort.

The nineteenth-century housewife, then, had fewer demands made upon her in at least two major spheres of activity, cleaning and cooking. She did not, however, idle her time away. Her work responsibilities typically extended beyond housework proper.

We have already seen that the fisherman's wife and the bleacher's wife were integral parts of the enterprise. Their daily tasks included tiring ones such as baiting hooks, repairing nets, or preparing linen strips for staking-out in the sun by sewing on small loops. They also had heavy tasks, such as hanging heavy nets or boiling linen. The three farmers' wives, too, had major outside duties. The so-called light work of the farm, especially harvesting, typically fell in part to them.

The wives of seamen, as well as others from poor families, often supplemented family income by occasional or part-time work, hiring out to farmer, fisherman, or bleacher to do the tasks their own women did. Some laundry and cleaning work could also be had in locally well-to-do homes, and a number of women worked in the local textile mill.

Occupational opportunities for the unmarried woman were limited. She might do housework or work at a vocation more or less tangential to housework, including school teaching, nursing, shopkeeping, or the textile mill.

Daughters ideally remained home until marriage, being apprenticed, as it were, to the mother. In the poorer households of fishermen and sailors, financial and other traditions might dictate a different type of domestic apprenticeship. According to old Danish custom, these girls worked as domestics in better-off homes in the village or elsewhere in Denmark. Much was expected of the young girl, who expected little in return. The first up in the mornings, she worked until she went to bed in the evening, except for every other Sunday when she was free—after two P.M. The hard, endless tasks were accepted as fitting and right. One taskmistress, for example, was considered unusually kind because she was generous about giving time off for festive occasions. She not only allowed her domestic to have the evening off to dance until six A.M. at the annual Shrovetide ball, but on coming back to work that morning the girl, after cleaning up the front room and making breakfast tea, was allowed to sleep until noon before taking up the routine of work again. The memory of such kindnesses remained with the girl until she was an old lady!

The educational benefits of working for a strange family were widely appreciated. It was also held that in some homes the domestic was not treated like a servant but rather like a member of the family, even though it is difficult to see any difference in the amount of work that was required. This difference in treatment was epitomized by the eating arrangements. To eat at the family dining room table rather than alone or with the cook in the kitchen placed the relationship between employer and employee on a higher level, enough so that girls from more highly placed families might also apprentice out as part of their training.

Of course modern women too work outside of the home. This, in fact, has come to include a far greater variety of employment than was the case in the nineties.

As the century progressed, education beyond the communal school level became more readily available to Dragorian girls, and the number of those who entered the teaching seminaries quadrupled by 1915. Candidates to nursing schools tripled during the same period. Copenhagen's first business school opened in 1909, and by 1912 Dragor had more than a dozen young women, several from upper-class homes, preparing for careers as office clerks and stenographers.

The village itself could not, of course, absorb the growing labor force of its young women. Teachers and nurses sought employment in Copenhagen, a situation that disturbed their families but little, since the tradition of "foreign" employment had long existed in these professions as well as for domestics, even for the daughters of the wealthy. The growing exodus of others to work in business houses and stores was accepted by extension. By this time, too, transportation developments made it feasible for women to maintain homes on the island but work in the city.

At the very end of the century in Dragor a few upper-class girls attended the semiprivate high school (*realskole*) in the village. During the course of the twentieth century, girls started to attend the university and technical schools of Copenhagen. To the surprise of many, they demanded purposeful study programs and the right to enter various professions. By the period subsequent to World War I, women were admitted to most professions formerly exclusively masculine, and by World War II it was no longer considered remarkable, even in Dragor, for a woman to be a physician, lawyer, dentist, engineer, or even a government official. This was a very rapid development from the first decade of the century when women were admitted only in limited numbers to a few professions where their lesser esteem was reflected in smaller pay relative to their male peers.

Many women still work as domestics, and there is a considerable hangover of attitude on the part of both employer and employee from the nineteenth century. They are still worked very hard and for long hours. Except under rare circumstances, they are regarded and spoken to as servants. In this respect, however, it must be noted that current employer-employee relations in general, and regardless of sex, are based on an attitude of sharp cleavage between superordinate and subordinate positions. Employers commonly treat their staffs brusquely and impersonally, receiving in return subservient deference and obsequiousness.

For the majority of the women, housekeeping and family care occupy most or all of their time.

Challenged by the growing complexity of homemaking, a number of young mothers formed the "Dragor's Housemothers Society" (*Dragørs Husmoders Forening*) in 1933, electing a panel of officers and writing into the minutes of their first meeting their goal of "mutual aid and encouragement in the art of raising a family." The society still meets, schedules speeches by specialists on everything from floral arrangements to foreign cooking, and has coffee together. Interest in the society is currently limited, however, to older women, the mothers of grown children, and to spinsters. Young mothers, no longer intimidated by technological and scientific innovation, are further disinclined to associate themselves with a society dominated by its charter members.

In this sketchy survey of the changing woman's world of Dragor we seem led to an obvious conclusion. The housewife, especially the mother of small children, was overworked in the nineties and she is overworked today.

Is there then no essential difference in the life of the Dragorian woman? Above all there has been a change in spiritual and intellectual life. We have noted the increased work imposed by modern standards of living. But modern standards also include homes with well-heated rooms, good light, and comfortable furniture. These provide the material basis for privacy. Whereas the nineteenth-century family had to spend their short evening hours together in the only room of the house that was heated and lighted, one may now retire to a warm room apart, where for longer periods one is free to read, to correspond, and to think quietly without being disturbed. At the same time, opportunities to utilize public libraries, to attend night courses in the local school, to visit fairs and museums, and ultimately to express oneself in a choice from a wide range of professions or leisure activities have increased and developed. Life now, for both men and women, is a far less brutal thing than it was in earlier decades. Self-realization is far more readily possible. This is the spiritual derivative of technological progress.[2]

[2] Professor Steensberg has drawn similar conclusions concerning the changing status of Danish peasants in his article "Bondens Hverdag," pp. 92–108.

5: The Young

Infancy

FAMILIES are smaller today in Dragor. In place of seemingly unlimited childbearing, few now have more than four children, and two or three are generally regarded as an ideal number.

For the prospective mother the daily routine continues virtually unchanged during early pregnancy. Unlike the older tendency to work until the day of delivery, modern working mothers usually leave their jobs during the last month or two. No shyness is felt about obvious bodily changes as was the case in the nineteenth century, but women do wear special maternity garments designed to enhance their appearance.

The national government has taken an increasing interest in the practice of medicine. The requirements for permission to practice as a midwife have been progressively stiffened. By 1920 it was necessary for a woman to study for one year in a special school for midwives. By 1945 an additional year of hospital internship in obstetrics was mandatory. During the thirties many Dragorian women began to make reservations for subsidized delivery in one of Copenhagen's several clinics. This practice has become more and more common, although there are still those who prefer to follow the old practice of remaining at home for childbirth. The reasons most commonly cited are that they prefer familiar surroundings to the strange decor and odors of the hospital, that they want their husbands to be present, and that they want to be assured of having their babies constantly at their disposition. Home births today, however, are attended by both the trained midwife and a physician, and in Dragorian homes as in

Copenhagen clinics anesthetics, medications, and instruments are used, where necessary, to ease the pain of labor and to facilitate delivery.

With the increasing refinements of national health insurance, it has become common to visit the physician frequently during pregnancy. The expectant mother is given a card with small coupons which indicate when she is to see the midwife for a series of periodic check-ups. In accordance with government health policies, nutrition is supervised from the first visit until long after the child is born.

For most Dragorians the cost of childbirth is met by national insurance or, if their income is too high for them to be included under its benefits, by a private insurance plan which is very popular. Women in lower-income groups are provided with a free half liter of milk daily during pregnancy and with a full liter during the postpartum nursing period.

In the 1890's, according to the standards of the well-to-do, the mother stayed in bed for fourteen days after parturition. Among the poor it was a matter of pride, and sometimes of necessity, to be up and about as soon as possible—after five or six days for the first birth, and in subsequent deliveries after three or four. Often it was difficult to get help in running the home during the period of convalescence. Sisters of the new parents were frequently unavailable because they had large families of their own, and even the parents' mothers might still have a houseful of youngsters. The help that came was generally sporadic and fortuitous. It was, however, customary for friends and neighbors to come with confinement dishes (*barselmad*), oatmeal soup or chicken soup, and the unusually good food made childbirth a joyful event for the other children in the family. A special women's party constituted the baby's introduction to society, even before his formal baptism a few days later.

During the contemporary new mother's first week at home neighbors visit, but usually just briefly. They do not ordinarily bring food. It is customary instead to present a little gift for the infant, often an article of clothing. The mother may well have the help of her own mother or a sister during the first week or two, since these women are not so likely to be burdened with children of their own as was the case in the nineteenth century. If no family help is available the state pays a professional housekeeper to take care of the family until the mother is able to resume her duties. In any case, the women's party has disappeared as an institutionalized practice, leaving the baptismal party as the usual rite of social presentation.

Dragorian mothers believe now as of old that it is best if an infant can stay on the breast for nine months to a year before weaning. Mothers now appear to have greater success in retaining their milk, an effort in which they are supported by national health instruction programs for prospective mothers and by the active assistance of the staffs of clinics and hospitals as well as of the public health nurses. There is enormous concern with diet. Hospitals allot special rations of milk, eggs, and malt beer, and the physician advises on home consumption. The advice of local residents continues to be that the nursing mother must eat enough for two.

There is a persistence of a former concern with "lumps" in the breasts. Formerly presumed to be the result of foolish practices such as putting hands in cold water, modern opinion finds its cause in the improper emptying of the breasts. This is alleviated, in accordance with the advice of the public health or hospital nurse, by alternating the breast on which feedings are begun, emptying one breast completely at each nursing before offering the child the second.

Female diseases were formerly regarded by most women as "natural" and unworthy of professional attention. The last decades, on the contrary, have witnessed an increasing tendency for women to consult specialists, generally being referred to them by the local physician.

Under the influence of pediatricians and trained midwives, infant feeding became more regularized after about 1930. This is especially the case during the baby's first week in the nursery of clinic or hospital, when feedings are fixed at four-hour intervals (with a two A.M. bottle replacing one breast feeding) and the infant is allowed to cry if hungry between feedings. Demand feeding, even for the mother with adequate help at home, has never been very popular, and most mothers try to follow the feeding schedule prescribed by their doctors and printed in a special booklet for new mothers. These schedules are not, however, without some elasticity, and mothers are cautioned to make the necessary adjustment if hunger cries are pronounced. Night feedings are allowed to end of their own accord when baby sleeps through them.

Vitamin drops are prescribed at the end of the first month; puréed vegetables, mashed banana, and specially processed cereals, at the fourth month ordinarily. Other fruits, egg yolk, and an increasing variety of mashed foods are gradually added from the sixth month, with scraped meat introduced late in the first year. As of old, the tendency is to get the baby on mashed (formerly premasticated) bits of the regular family food.

The general attitude toward toilet training is casual as of old, with shaming and light spankings still administered by many mothers to persistent offenders.

During his first year of life, a child is visited fifteen times by the public health nurse, whose services are paid for from the national treasury. She examines and weighs the child on each visit, prescribes treatment for minor ailments, such as colic or skin rash, and refers the child or the mother to the physician in more serious cases. The child is also given free examinations, at the discretion of the physician, at the public school. Vaccinations are begun at the end of the first year.

Infant care contrasts to nineteenth-century practices, pervasively apparent, are neatly epitomized by comparing any aspect of modern infant hygiene with the obsolete pacifier made by placing prechewed bread and sugar in a gauze cone. If the modern baby's world seems less personal and overregulated, at least he has a far greater likelihood of surviving it.

Childhood: Work and Play

From infancy to age fourteen the child gradually extended its activities from cradle and house until it had the run of the village, its hours occupied with play, chores, and school.

Money was but rarely spent on games and toys, but it seems that children never lack entertainment when water is at hand. In the summer, every child not otherwise occupied spent the warm hours of the day swimming, boys off the southern mole, girls farther down the beach at a small pier called *knudens bro*. The latter wore home-made costumes of linen or cotton covering them well from neck to ankle. Boys swam naked, always putting on their caps when emerging from the water, for if it did not protect modesty it was at least reputed to help immensely to keep warm in the cooling breeze.

It was not difficult to beg or borrow a trap or a few hooks to do a little fishing, and with a bit of luck a few øre might be earned on the catch. Sometimes boys helped the men at the harbor for the pure joy of it. When the kindling boat unloaded, a bit of help was rewarded with the privilege of using the rowboat for a while. Older boys sometimes succeeded in borrowing a boat to which they could attach a small improvised sail, but they risked punishment if they were foolhardy enough to venture beyond the protection of the inner harbor. Another activity was to sail model ships, hand-made. A good father saw to it that his son had one that was trim and seaworthy.

Forms of play changed with the seasons. In winter wooden ice skates were strapped to the bottoms of shoes, and activities extended to the frozen beach and inland pond. On occasions when the ice was smooth, skaters used a hand-made, kitelike sail to race with the wind along the frozen beach. Winter also gave opportunity to use the wooden sled a father or grandfather had made.

Away from the water, time passed with other things. In the irregular streets and houses and the surrounding meadows and park, make-believe soldiers chased make-believe robbers. Boys industriously constructed kites, bows and arrows, and crossbows to be used in fields and streets, while girls were occupied with dressing dolls and playing house.

Here and there children played at games of skill and chance. In the game, *at nipse med pinde* one stick was used to bat another stick into the air, the object being to hit the stick as high as possible and still catch it. In *at stikke,* two-øre pieces were thrown toward a line drawn on the ground. The winner, he who threw closest to the line, then tossed all of the coins into the air and was allowed to keep those that landed headside up. In a second throw, all landing heads up went to the boy who placed second, and so on. In a similar type of game using coins or brass buttons, the first player threw his button and the others had to throw theirs on top of it. The one who came closest, if it were no farther away than the length of a match, took the buttons and was the first to throw in the next round. Children also gambled with their collections of the glass-headed pins which women used to hold their Amager dresses in place.

The above games were played mostly by boys, who left *at bikle* to the girls. This game, in a form characteristic of Amager, was played with three to five small sheep bones which had been colored by boiling with Easter eggs in water and rotten onions. The girls took turns, the trick being to throw a small glass or iron ball in the air, pick up successively one to five bones lying on the ground and then catch the ball with the same hand. This done, the player tossed the ball up again, and threw the bones in the same order through a bridge made on the ground by the thumb and index finger of the other hand, again catching the ball before it landed. In the third and final throw, the object was to pick up the bones with the knuckles. While taking her turn, the player was also supposed to sing the following ditty, which is an un-intelligible mixture of Dutch and Danish words.

Bøjen løj densov, densov	Fire ke duseldanker,
Smurt en forenfugl,	Datein to forgæves,
en kenobrek,	Een to alle dage,
to kenastik,	Een to alle dinge,
tre kenu forliser,	Een to forgæves.

But life was not all play for children, especially in poor families. Children were expected to fetch water, buy bread at the baker's, fill the milk pitcher at the farmer's, or empty the privy buckets at a village midden. The latter job was always performed after dark, and was referred to circuitously as "going to Tivoli" (the amusement center in Copenhagen). Boys had an exclusive domain in heavier jobs such as sawing wood in the fall and fetching sand for cleaning floors, while girls were recruited for assistance in housekeeping and care of siblings.

Some chores contributed significantly to the family income. Thus, all children went to the nearby farms with a handcart to glean cabbages and potatoes. They might also search the commons for goose eggs. In families where the women wove, children might have the daily task of winding spools with thread.

Some chores provided a chance for minor entrepreneurs. In the fall, boys collected seaweed in addition to the amount needed to cover their family's winter supply of cabbage, selling it by the cartload to farmers. In the winter boys chopped through the ice of the Sound to dig sand which could be sold for two øre a bucketful to people without children of their own. Extra cabbages or potatoes might be collected and peddled. In the summer children as well as adult women might help fishermen, between six and eight A.M. before school, cleaning hooks and lines (at four *øre* per hundred hooks) and again, between four and six P.M., baiting hooks and placing them in trays. Occasionally a boy would buy forty herring for a couple of *øre* a piece and sell them in the village for a profit of twenty or thirty øre.

Steady, part-time employment was also common. Girls sometimes worked half days as domestics from the age of eleven or twelve. Boys found jobs as *bydrenge* for stores and craft shops, delivering goods, performing simple tasks, and cleaning the establishment. Within the family, a boy frequently worked part time without salary as a partner to his father in fishing or worked as an apprentice in the father's craft.

Child labor was relied upon in almost every functioning, domestic family. In some cases, it was simply a matter of relieving adults of tiresome but light duties, but among the poor it was often an important part of providing income for the family, either directly as labor in the father's or mother's occupation, or indirectly by earning room, board, and/or money elsewhere.

The children's world had its own social structure, which disappeared in the new century. All children between seven and fourteen years belonged to either "the north end" (*nordenden*) or "the south end" (*sydenden*), membership depending upon whether residence was north or south of the midvillage street called Gothersgade (modern Von Ostensgade). Girls and boys restricted their nonschool associations to members of their own half of town. The two groups were rivals. At times, although not always, the trespassing of a young person from the other side of the dividing street was contested, and a number of times a year, particularly in the winter, the two groups met in combat, fighting with snowballs or even sticks. The fights usually ended with the routing of one side, the defeated combatants disappearing into their homes, or with the dispersal of both sides when one boy appeared to be more or less seriously injured. Adults did not participate in north-south hostilities, nor were they influenced by them in their own social relations. It is notable, however, that to a certain degree, the moieties divided wealthier families from poorer ones.

In the twentieth century the Dragorian child found the horizons of his world extended significantly beyond the village and Amager Island. Today every child has been to Copenhagen. Many go frequently, to visit relatives, to play at Tivoli, to be outfitted with new clothes, to see holiday decorations in the store windows of Strøjet Street. As the children grow older and can make trips to Copenhagen on their own, knowledge of city life becomes more intimate.

In Dragor water is still a prime source of amusement for the young, but homemade, hand-fashioned toys have been replaced by factory-made boats, plastic beach balls and buckets, and machine-made metal ice skates. Boys and girls swim together now, and, except for a few naked toddlers, all wear modern bathing suits.

Sail skating no longer occurs, but in the summer roller skates are popular. The games, *at bikle* and *at nipse med pinde* have disappeared, and there remains only a simpler form of *at stikke,* but there are also new diversions. Organized street games enjoy periods of fadlike popularity shared by town and city youngsters alike, to fall suddenly from favor and be replaced by a new diversion that catches the fancy of a few and spreads like wildfire through a peer group. "I spy," a game that combined guessing and tag was popular in the spring of 1957, suddenly to be replaced by a new version of the old hopscotch game—"Hens and Flowers"—in which the participants are matched in teams.

Chores have changed. Today children clean yards and run to the store and generally have less difficult tasks to perform, now that it is no longer necessary to empty privies, carry water, and saw wood. Not infrequently children are given a small money allowance each week to be used as they wish or to be saved. Many families give these allowances on the understanding that they represent payment for the performance of weekly or daily chores.

Part-time employment for children is also less arduous than formerly, and is rarely reckoned a part of the family budget. Most jobs are taken at the desire of the child (more commonly the boys) to earn money for things they would not otherwise be able to have—particular clothes, toys, or a new bicycle. The jobs available are mostly as errand boys for stores, including morning delivery of milk, bread, newspapers, and the like. There is some casual employment to be had in helping neighbors with light chores around the house and yard.

Children, in sum, have lost their importance in the family economy. The time formerly devoted to work has not shifted to play, however, but to school.

Childhood: School

The Dragorian child of the nineties normally attended part-time school. Paid school (*betalingsskole*), the private enterprise of one or another old maid or widow, took youngsters between four or five and seven years of age. The school met six mornings a week from nine to eleven-thirty. Not all children attended, largely because it cost the parents one crown a month, and those who did were generally sent in order to free busy mothers for other work. Nonetheless, the school was a serious business. There were no walks, there was no singing, and there were no toys to play with, although the teacher read Bible stories or fairy tales during the last part of the daily period. Otherwise, each child had a small blackboard and a piece of chalk and the time was spent learning to write and to do arithmetic. These subjects were later relearned in the communal school for older children, but it was felt that the children profited from an early beginning.

The communal school, for children between the ages of seven and fourteen, was housed in three brick buildings built respectively in 1827, 1860, and 1891. In response to a law of 1882 which fined parents for absenteeism, Dragorians of the 1890's had fully abandoned the former practice of keeping their children out of school. The law, however, was not enforced so strictly that children were not occasionally absent for causes other than the acceptable one of ill health, particularly at seasons when parents required their help at their work.

The communal school had three teachers—two men and one woman. Each had a morning class and an afternoon class. The teachers were appointed by the communal council and had prepared themselves for their vocation by attending one of the nation's schools for teacher training. One of the teachers was appointed head (*overlærer*), and had the responsibility for administering the school and supervising the curriculum. Teachers were paid out of a special communal fund, their meager salary significantly increased by the "part" they received from the profits of ship salvage.

The atmosphere of the classroom was strict for the children, tedious for the teachers, and not very far removed from the world beyond the red-brick building. The men teachers smoked in the classroom, and all had to take care of practical matters, in addition to instruction, or suffer the consequences. A can of kerosene was kept handy for treating dry rot or cleaning the coal stove. A student whose habits of personal hygiene were far from the optimum in cleanliness might be cautioned to care for himself, and there were packaged remedies for the treatment of hair lice. Sulphur matches were kept at hand and lit, when necessary, to counteract offensive odors. Pupils and teacher shared the same bucket toilet, whose slanting seat was designed to discourage loiterers. Wooden shoes of daily wear were left at the door, and in the classroom cloth slippers were worn by the students. The teachers, however, usually wore leather shoes, a distinction of professional people. They were not, however, above utilizing the labor force of their charges for running errands, fetching kindling for their homes as well as the school, or tending their geese.

Girls and boys sat in separate classes, the boys having men teachers and the girls usually taught by the women. Children attended classes every day but Sunday for half a day, either in the morning from eight-thirty to eleven-thirty or in the afternoon from twelve-thirty to three-thirty. Generally, classes numbered about twenty-five pupils. Instruction was free, but children had to buy their own books.

Instruction under these circumstances varied considerably according to the individual teacher's personality and motivation, although textbooks standard to all of Denmark as well as a generally accepted choice of subject matter matter fostered some uniformity.

The school history of one girl serves to illustrate the formal education Dragorian children received at the end of the nineteenth century. In her first class, when she was seven years old, she had a strict, elderly spinster. This was a morning period and the order of the day was singing of songs, including national, folk and church songs from "The Children's Song Book for School and Home" (*Børnesangbog for skolen og hjemmet*) followed by reading and finally, arithmetic. Homework did not begin for another year or two, but a pupil got a pinch on the arm for not remembering the lesson from the preceding day. When the teacher was inclined she read either adventure or Bible stories.

In second class, also morning scheduled, our informant got a new teacher, a spinster from Copenhagen. The former teacher had retired because of old age. Instruction in reading, writing, and arithmetic was supplemented by training in the practical arts of sewing, darning, and knitting. (Boys received comparable training in the use of carpenter tools.) In the third class, meeting in the afternoons, our informant got a new teacher again, a young woman from the peninsula of Jutland who created quite a stir in the village. This was 1899 and the young teacher was the first woman in the community to ride a bicycle, which was considered quite distressing by many of the local inhabitants. The old women who still wore the national costume particularly regarded bike riding as unthinkable. Instruction was in reading, writing, and arithmetic, and, as much as for the bicycle, the teacher was ridiculed by the townsmen for adding gymnastics to the curriculum for girls and teaching it herself. There was no handwork, but there was regular religious instruction through Bible stories and the memorization of songs, verses, and the catechism.

The fourth class did not differ essentially from the third except that it met in the mornings. In the fifth class, meeting in the afternoons, the informant had a man for a teacher, a South Jutlander. He was strongly interested in natural history, lecturing on the recognition of plants and trees, and on the history of the disputed border area from which he had originated. Children learned the patriotic Danish songs which were sung in his home province and, more formally, were instructed in Danish grammar, world history, free-style writing and religion. The sixth and seventh classes were morning classes with the same man, and did not differ greatly from the fifth in organization, except that geography was added in the last year. In the seventh class no meeting was held on Friday mornings in order to permit the pupils to attend the one-hour confirmation class in the parsonage.

The activities of the communal school exceeded the compulsory class requirements largely because of the personal initiative of many of the teachers. Thus, the teacher from Southern Jutland collected books from local residents and, together with his own collection, formed a lending library much utilized by the children, especially to provide reading materials for the long winter evenings. During the winter the head teacher taught evening school classes for young people ten to fourteen years of age, charging a very nominal fee. The classes met three times a week from five to seven P.M. and presented such subject matter as arithmetic, writing, physics (which was not taught in the regular school), handicrafts, dancing, and drawing. The period always ended with the reading of stories by the teachers, often short stories by foreign as well as Danish authors. Instruction was not intensive and the pupils attended largely for the diversion it provided.

In addition to the preschool-age classes there were several other educational facilities functioning for the most part independently of the communal government and providing instruction as a form of private enterprise. They were, nevertheless, considered as much a part of the educational system as the communal school. One such school was conducted by an old Sound pilot. Pupils from the third and fourth classes of the communal school attended the pilot's class during the half day free from regular school. Here they were intensively taught arithmetic and writing. Most important of these private schools was that of a middle-aged man who held a degree (*Cand. Phil.*) from the University of Copenhagen. This school was, in effect, the local high school (*realskole*) and received a small amount of money from communal funds to permit the teacher to take in some of the village's most promising boys of poor families at half price and sometimes free of charge. The class was for children eleven to fourteen years old and about twenty boys from well-to-do families made up the bulk of students attending during the part of the day free from communal school. The meeting place was one room of the teacher's apartment in a home in the center of town, and the room's furnishings consisted of no more than tables, chairs, small blackboards and chalk. Instruction was in English, German, world history, zoology, botany, mathematics, and physics—instruction essential to those who hoped to attend the navigation school in Copenhagen. Although the school was primarily intended for boys aspiring to ship's officer or pilot, several girls also attended at the end of the decade. As in the communal school, no examinations were given, but pupils were seated according to the quality of their work, the best in the front seats. In addition, report cards were given out, the grade for each week recorded and submitted to parents on Saturdays.

Girls did not ordinarily attend the *realskole,* but those of better-off families attended sewing class from one to four in the after-

noon, conducted by a local woman in her parlor. Under her tute-
lage young ladies learned fine sewing, embroidery, and knitting.

The outstanding changes in twentieth century Dragorian schooling lie in the increasingly dominant role of public schools in a
child's life and in the increasing uniformity of subject matter and
teaching methods. Of former private and semiprivate schools only
a vestige remains. Two middle-aged women take preschool children into their homes for the forenoon. These "kindergartens"
(*børnehave*), as they are called, are very sparsely attended by
those children who could not be admitted to the oversubscribed
communal nursery for working mothers. The "teacher" makes no
systematic effort to teach, but acts in fact simply as a baby sitter,
taking her charges on long walks, on personal errands, or allowing them freedom to play while she is occupied with her housework.

A more tangible descendant of the paid school is a nursery
financed by the communal government and supervised by the
committee on schools. A response to the rising needs of working
mothers for inexpensive care for children between the ages of
three and seven years, the nursery gives orientational instruction
in reading and provides food and play facilities, as well as regular
medical examinations.

The communal school has been housed since 1955 in a large
building designed to meet the specific needs of its pupils. Class-
rooms are airy and cheerful, plumbing facilities are designed for
children, and specialized accommodations are provided for activities such as music and athletics. The school even includes an
auditorium, a dining room, a doctor's office where the physician
is to be found several times a week, and a dentist's office where a
lady dentist and her assistant are in daily attendance.

Since 1910 the school has had to conform to progressively more
explicit rules of the National Ministry of Education. The staff
now consists of a school inspector, who administers the school
and teaches fifteen hours a week, an assistant school inspector,
thirteen regular teachers (of whom three are classed as head
teachers), and two part-time teachers. Salaries are fixed and paid
by the community, and are kept equal to those of Copenhagen in
view of the propinquity of the town to the capital. Teachers no
longer receive money gifts from their students at Confirmation,
nor part of the profits of salvage.

Students number 540 and classes are now coeducational except for craft work, home-making classes, and physical education after the third year. The subjects taught and the methods used are specifically defined and outlined in a mimeographed handbook edited by the school inspector and approved by the Ministry of Education. Following national law, the curriculum conforms to a program of studies ubiquitously enforced throughout Denmark. This uniformity is a response to the demands of an urban environment, where young people applying for work to strangers must have a readily comprehensible documentation of their training, and where higher schools, professional schools, and the university must be able to plan courses on the basis of a uniform background for all entrants regardless of place of origin within Denmark.

After the first five years, called "basic school" (*grundskole*), pupils make a major life's decision in the selection of which of two curricula they will follow. The "nonexamination middle school" (*eksamensfri mellemskole*) corresponds a great deal to the old communal school curriculum and is completed in three years when the child is fourteen or fifteen years of age. The second of the curricula is the "examination middle school" of four years' duration, which may at the option of the pupil be followed by the high school (*realskole*) program of an additional four years. An examination at the end of the first year of high school, the *real eksamen,* qualifies the student for many jobs, including many civil-service positions. The examination at the end of high school, the *studentereksamen,* must be passed for admission to the university and to other professional schools, and is for many an educational goal in itself.

Extracurricular activities are today a function of the school rather than of teachers as individuals. Year-round evening courses at a small charge offer subjects appealing to youth and adults, ranging from pottery-making, art, and cooking to mathematics, typewriting, history, and foreign languages. This program also includes the presentation of five or six travel films during the winter for which admission is free.

The school cooperates with two independent clubs that function to organize the nonschool hours of children and youth. *Dragør Boldklub* (Dragor Ball Club) has flourished since its founding after the turn of the century and now possesses a modern clubhouse in addition to its sports fields and tennis courts, attracting sports-interested young people of both sexes. *Ungdomsklub* (Youth Club) supported by the communal government, was founded in 1955 to provide game and social rooms for local youngsters in an effort to keep them off the streets in the evenings. The Boy Scouts and the Girl Scouts, meeting in the school or at the Youth Club, are of primary interest to school-age children. During the first part of the century an activity limited to the children of "fine folk," it now provides healthy activity for many children of all socioeconomic levels.

To summarize, as the adult world has changed since the end of the last century, the child's world and his preparation for maturity have also changed. Play will always be important. To some extent it functions to prepare the child for adulthood, and thus the modern child becomes familiar with motors and plastics as well as with ships and sails. But the more direct learning of a trade or profession has dramatically shifted from an emphasis upon early work participation in a subordinate capacity to complete dependence upon formal schooling. This transition was made effortlessly as older school practices were slowly but persistently elaborated and expanded and as increasing prosperity allowed the family budget to adapt. As a result of this shift, modern technological know-how is efficiently inculcated in the young. In this way, too, modern habits of regularity and punctuality— the new work rhythms—are learned where time vagueness formerly ruled. And finally, partly through school the child gains a reality orientation that extends beyond village, region, and nation to include the world in its entirety.

6: And the Old

THE time when one joined the ranks of the elderly was not formally marked in old Dragor. Retirement parties did not occur. One became old gradually, almost imperceptibly. Women found that their work lessened quite naturally and gradually as their children grew up and left home, the nature of their work remaining basically homemaking. Men, as time went on, gave up more strenuous work, occupied themselves with occasional fishing on a small scale, with running a small home shop, or doing odd jobs for other villagers. Old skippers and pilots might take office as mayor or councilman or communal functionary.

For some old men it was difficult to quit the sea and the familiar, active way of life. The turning point for these men was often a debilitating disease, an accidental injury, or encroaching physical disability, which forced them to enter into a more sedentary job or restricted their full participation in their regular vocation.

But whether forced to give up more virile pursuits or happy to do so, the major concern of the old was a financial one. Their needs were not great, however, and often were met by savings and property benefits or by the assistance of their sons. Among the poor, an old couple could usually get by on the small amount of labor, fishing, or gleaning they still could do. A few jobs were traditionally reserved for the old, such as that of village watchman and harbor master. An old widow could manage with the help of salvage money, and perhaps the revenue from a bit of home weaving or from selling fish.

Those who could not get support in any other way had ultimate recourse to the village poor house (*fattiggaard*). Mostly men, the inmates were locked in every day of the week except Sundays when they were permitted to leave the premises or to receive visits from friends and relatives. They occupied themselves with small tasks as their ability permitted, caring for the house and yard, unraveling old rope to make calking material for ships, doing simple carpentry. Their standard of living depended partly upon the man paid by the community to act as supervisor (*økenom*). If he were careful, wise, and unselfish he fed them fairly well on the funds available. Inevitably, however, their standard of living was very low and their possessions absolutely minimal.

Often, of course, physical ailments, unalleviated by effective medical treatment, were a cruel burden to bear. But, despite its inescapable handicaps, old age had its compensations. The old man or woman normally had a place in the life of his fellow villagers as a source of occasional help in minor jobs, in the relationship group as the helpful grandparent, and as the focal point for the kin group, especially at holidays. They lived in a village known intimately since childhood and which, in spite of the changes of the nineteenth century, was still not greatly different from their earliest days. In the summer, the old men passed their time at the harbor, comparing the ships and fish hauls to their own exploits, often embellished by the passing of time, occupied and comfortable and accepted amid familiar surroundings and activities.

As men left the sea to take employment in the city, the gradual entrance into old age was replaced by a sudden and dramatic one. A person became old when he was retired from his job, sometimes involuntarily by company regulation, the event signaled usually by a retirement party. For many the transition from active to inactive status was demoralizingly abrupt. Although happier than many of their urban age mates for the solace of intimate surroundings and the diversions of the harbor, only a few can occupy themselves readily with casual fishing, farming, or light harbor jobs, and activities such as gleaning and assisting the bleachers have disappeared. Their families are often widely scattered during the day, and even their youngest grandchildren are occupied in government-supported nursery schools especially geared, it would seem, to render grandparents superfluous.

With the progress of twentieth-century medicine, old age is less subject to disease and suffering than of old, and improved government pension support has minimized the financial problem formerly met by minor enterprise. Yet few men and women are able to make the old, casual adjustment. The problem of isolation and of lack of purpose is serious; sufficiently so to warrant the conclusion that of all age levels, the old alone seem seriously to have suffered in the process of urbanization.

7: Making a Living

Former Semisubsistence Economy

THE occupations that established the tone of life in Dragør had their economic orientation in a money economy. The return on labor was either a wage or a salable commodity. Nonetheless, the poor especially had a large degree of independence of money. Much fish was eaten costing nothing for the fisherman and purchased cheaply by others, especially by those who went to the harbor to bargain for the few mackerel, cod, or flounder that turned up in eel traps in amounts too small for ordinary marketing, or for the bony fish (*aalekvappe*) which city people did not deign to eat. Fishermen, including seamen home in the fall, caught and salted some eel and herring for storage in large barrels for winter use. Amagerian farmers traditionally allowed free gleaning of their fields to the villagers, and this often yielded all of a family's needs in potatoes and cabbages.

Villagers kept domestic animals and fowl in addition to their main occupations. So many people kept geese that Dragør gained a national reputation for having large flocks wandering freely about. Many Dragorians had small coops at the water's edge where geese, ducks, and chickens were kept. Others had coops in their yards, and a few used a room in the house for this purpose. In spring the village geese were ferried to the island of Saltholm where they were left to take care of themselves for the summer. Sometimes they swam home themselves when the summer drew to an end, their arrival bringing the whole village to the beach. Each owner then sought out his own by checking the property marks: small wedges clipped from the webbed feet in patterns unique to each man. In winter, when they spent their nights, at least, sheltered in coop or room, and when they could not feed entirely on the meadows, they were kept alive with small amounts of purchased grain plus scraps from the table. In the fall, the so-called "Køge-wagon" (from the town of Køge, Sealand) visited the village. Its arrival was soon known to all of the geese owners, who brought their fall-fat birds to sell. Carted off, then, to market in Copenhagen and Roskilde, they left their former owners with a bit of money for the winter—not a lot of money, to be sure, but in any case "a good shilling to have," a few being able to support themselves entirely from it.

In addition to the extra income, geese provided eggs, and an occasional stew that a family could sup on for upwards of a week. During the molting period, many villagers arose before dawn to collect pinfeathers on the meadows for blanket and pillow stuffing. A goose that fell sick and died could not be eaten, but at least its down could be salvaged. The story is told of a poor rheumatic villager, too crippled to do much other than care for his geese. He found some pain relief in applying rags soaked in *aquavitæ* to his aching limbs. One afternoon, if we are to believe the story, he found two of his geese dead, which left him no alternative but to pluck them, and throw the bodies on the midden. To his astonishment, the next day he saw two naked geese foraging with his flock. The poor creatures had not been dead, but simply intoxicated from nibbling at the old man's discarded *aquavitæ* poultice.

Scraps from the table also fed the pig or two that might be kept, these beasts otherwise providing for themselves by scavenging in the drainage ditches and at the village middens. Others kept sheep, which sustained themselves on the village meadows and provided an income from their wool as well as their meat. The meadow also helped feed the family cow, which provided milk for drinking, making of butter, or for hot buttermilk soup. All of the cows were cared for during the day by a village herder, who received a tiny sum for each animal in his care. Every morning and evening the herder with his horn led his charges in procession through the village between meadow and house. Returning home in the evening the herd diminished in size as it crept along the street, each animal turning without cue to follow the path from the main street to its stall.

Two significant items of diet were purchased: oats for morning cereal, and black, rye bread, since Dragorian women seldom used their ovens. Other more or less dispensable purchases included sugar, coffee and tea, salt and spices.

All clothes were handmade from shoes to caps—or could be at any rate. A man's Sunday clothes as well as the everyday seaman's visor cap, men's and women's leather shoes, worn mostly only to church or party, and the fine French shawls the ladies wore to festive events were purchased from stores in Copenhagen or the shoemaker in the village. For the most part, however, even the well-to-do wore clothes sewn, knitted, and embroidered by the adult women in the family, kept for long periods of time by subsequent care in mending and patching. Clothing purchases were largely limited to raw materials: wool yarn, thread, and cloth. Even cloth might be hand-loomed in the home, since the old home-weaving industry was still in existence, although it became clear during this decade that it could not compete with the weaving factory which had been established on the outskirts of the village in 1887. In 1890 there were 112 home looms in Dragor at which women supplemented the income of sea-going spouses. Indeed, the loom was considered a normal part of the sitting-room furniture. While the mother was at the loom the small children played around her or sat next to her on the bench, gradually learning to help as they grew older. A regular job for children in these homes was to wind the thread on spools, enough to last for a day taking a couple of hours. Eventually, a second loom might be added when a daughter was old enough to work at it. Although not ordinarily found in the homes of the better-off, they were almost inevitable in a widow's dwelling, for this was the most common answer to the lack of life insurance in a community where almost every family knew intimately what it meant to lose a father, son, husband, or brother at sea. When a new piece of cloth was begun, three or four women—aunts, grandmothers, or neighbors—were needed to help and the job was followed by a little party with coffee, thick cream, and cakebread. A small family celebration was also called for when a piece was finished, but the refreshments were minimal, for the profit was no more than a couple of pennies (øre) a yard if the cloth were sold, and much of it was destined for the market in Copenhagen. So small was the profit that the weaver could not afford to ride into town to sell it, but was forced to walk, leaving early in the morning. Pride demanded that shoes be worn to town—leather shoes—but economy dictated that they too be carried once Store Magleby was passed, bare feet sufficing for the greater part of the journey.

In addition to food and clothing there was the cost of shelter. Many of the poorest owned their own little cottage, having bought it at marriage with money saved and borrowed. Their housing expenses were but slight, the debt being long-term, property taxes being absent, and the least durable part of the house, the straw roof, put on by specialists from Sealand, lasting for fifty to seventy-five years. Others rented, paying forty to sixty crowns a year, due every six months on the "devil's birthday." Some of the heating and cooking could be with wood found along the beach, but otherwise money was needed for the purchase of firewood, which came from Sweden, and coal from even farther abroad. Most families bought the winter supply of wood in late fall from a skipper who sold it directly from his ship. Boys helped the skipper unload for the privilege of using his rowboat in the harbor, and later had the job of sawing the wood over a period of weeks in the attic of the home, where inclement weather could not interfere. Neither coal nor wood could be banked at night in the iron stoves, which meant a saving of fuel costs but also subjected people to sleeping in a veritable icebox when midwinter arrived.

In the absence of gas and electricity light came from petroleum lamps, but expenditures were kept to a minimum by not lighting the lamp until the evening meal at 6:30 and going to bed when the lamp burned low. In addition to petroleum, candles were also purchased and sparingly used. Small-handled lanterns burning a single candle were always carried at night by women walking out-of-doors, for the streets were very dark in the long winter nights, lit only by an occasional lamp placed at a street corner and tended by the night watchman, or by the small cracks of light from windows shuttered against the northern cold. Even with a candle, the streets, poorly drained, poorly cobbled, with open drainage ditches and occasional debris, were an adventure after dark.

Water cost nothing, but had to be pumped by hand from wells. Most houses had their own pumps, but since water was often poor, a daily chore of the family sons was to fetch water at one of the town pumps, that at the school reputedly yielding the sweetest water. Making two or three trips a day carrying two buckets suspended from a wooden shoulder yoke, a youngster's most discouraging accident was to slip on ice and spill the water just before pouring it into the storage barrel.

With the possibility of supplying most needs by personal industry, and with the absence of taxes due to the town's income from salvaging, a Dragorian in the nineties could obtain a minimal standard of living in most years if his health were good. Many suffered from poverty because even this minimal work opportunity was absent. These were the aged and infirm and the chronic alcoholics. Distilled potato liquor (locally called *snaps* or *brandtvin* and more broadly known as *aquavitæ*), beer, and imported rum were extremely cheap. A number of families lost not only their ready cash, but, far worse, the health and industry of their providers to the easy availability of alcoholic drink.

The Modern Importance of Money

But if life was often difficult for the nineteenth-century Dragorian, its demands were then more feasibly met on a limited income than is the case today. The independence of money that was so prevalently important in the old organization of the village economy has ceased to exist.

Fish is still a popular item of diet, and the fisherman supplies his family from his catch, but it is no longer customary for fish to be given to the poor or sold for practically nothing at the harbor. Fishermen no longer salt down a barrel of eel or herring for winter provisions. On today's market, this would be too great a luxury, for these fish command a high price and are sold when caught. Other, cheaper food must be purchased during the cold months.

Except for fowl, domestic animals have disappeared as a source of food or revenue. When Copenhageners started living in Dragor after 1907 they objected strongly to the dirt, smell, and nuisance of pigs running in the streets, and their objections were echoed by many of the indigenous inhabitants who decided that they, too, were much annoyed by it all. By 1920, pigs had virtually disappeared. Cows ceased to be kept about the same time. When fresh bottled milk could be had at reasonable prices by people now much more accustomed to a money economy, the investment and trouble which cows represented seemed scarcely to repay itself. Nor was there continued interest in keeping sheep.

Dragor, however, is still known as the town of geese. Twenty-three families have chickens and geese in their backyards, and many more keep them in coops on the meadow by the water. They no longer enjoy the run of the house. The keeping of fowl is generally regarded as a hobby, and most people keep only a few to provide a special dinner for the family or an extra bit of income. Some residents, mostly fishermen, keep flocks of twenty to fifty geese as a profitable if nonessential enterprise which provides a welcome supplement to their income when the birds are delivered in the fall to a wholesale buyer in Copenhagen. The geese themselves would find little changed in their way of life. They are still taken to Saltholm island in the summer; they wander the streets freely when in Dragor; their feet are still clipped. The pinfeathers that fall in the fields, however, are no longer retrieved for blankets and pillows. The effort involved is considered too great a price for the reward realized. Today it is far more reasonable to earn the price of a good pillow at another task.

Around 1947, fowl, particularly geese, occupied the conversations of many Dragorians. There were complaints that ducks and geese sullied the streets from their promenades, blocked traffic when they wandered onto the main streets, and were generally noisy and a public nuisance. The condition of their beach coops provoked the greatest criticism, however. There were rumors, indeed, that these symbols of Dragorian integrity would soon be outlawed by the communal council. Responding to the problem, the hen, duck, and geese keepers formed a society, "Dragor Fowl Association" (*Dragør Fjærkræ Forening*) with a set of rules and a governing body of three officers—a foreman, treasurer, and a representative. These officers, on behalf of the new society, met with the communal council and discussed the problem. The result was that the council promised that fowl would not be outlawed so long as the society was able to rectify the sources of complaint. It was, in particular, agreed to rent to the society a section of the public meadow by the beach where all coops should be concentrated and supervised by the society. Now every keeper of fowl using the meadow must be a member of the society, or of a second one formed since and having its plot farther south. Members pay a small fee each year and are subject to the rules

XAVIER UNIVERSITY LIBRARY
NEW ORLEANS, LA. 70125

of the society which limit the number of fowl which may be kept to ten hens, fifteen ducks or geese, and twenty-five new-born birds. Fowl keeping is not to be made a profession, and these maximums were fixed in a joint meeting of the Dragor Fowl Association and the council. Once a year a general meeting of association members is held at which problems are discussed and complaints settled. Members whose coops do not meet the society's standards of cleanliness are cautioned under threat of fine. At this meeting officers are elected. Tenure is for two years, one officer elected in even-numbered years, the other two in odd-numbered years. Attendance, however, appears largely stimulated by the social diversions afforded to members, and funds remaining from the year's expenses are utilized for a beer party limited to members' families. The harbor coops have been cleaned up, but ducks and geese still block traffic and no solution was found to the unpleasant remains of their promenades or their occasional noise. There are still complaints, but large-scale protest has been assuaged.

The occasional Dragorian who has an apple tree in his garden generally preserves some of its fruit on trays in his attic, but otherwise, townspeople today do not stock fresh produce against the winter, buying, instead, as need dictates, from the stores. During World War I when food prices rose precipitously, Amager farmers put an end to the gleaning of potatoes and cabbages, choosing to strip the fields themselves. The custom of allowing gleaners into the fields was never resumed.

During the last fifty years there has been a steadily increasing trend to greater and greater use of purchased, ready-made clothes. This was particularly the case for men, whose fine clothes were already factory-made in the nineties and whose work clothes soon afterwards came to be. By the 1920's knitted sweaters and socks were all that remained handmade, and by 1930 even they were largely replaced by purchased articles. Some of the old people, however, knit to this day the dark brown or grey wool socks held superior to anything that can be purchased. Women and girls have been slower to turn to ready-made clothes, and in present-day "Old Town" it is still very common for ladies of all classes to wear garments made by themselves, by a member of the family, or—if they haven't the time or skill—by a seamstress.

Home weaving has now completely disappeared as a home

industry although a few modern women have revived it as a hobby, sometimes reproducing the old textile patterns as an artistic enterprise. The girls of the nineties were the last to be apprenticed to the craft, and they gave it up as unprofitable during the first decade of the twentieth century. Many turned instead to work in the weaving mill. A few of the older women continued at home weaving, though it was underpaid, simply because it was easier to continue at something familiar than to find other employment. When these few died off between the two world wars, the home-weaving industry came to an end.

Until well into the twentieth century, those Dragorians who did not own their little homes rented them for a small enough sum so that payments were seldom a problem of major proportions. After the completion of the railroad in 1907, however, a few well-to-do Copenhageners began to build large villas along the north beach of the town. This was the beginning of a trend. During the course of fifty years the number of these villas grew steadily, augmented by the efforts of upper-class Dragorians who began to construct houses in the same area and in the same style. But housing itself did not come to present a serious problem until the second world war when the severe shortage of accommodations in Copenhagen sent city people into the surrounding countryside for places to live. Bus service was improved and every spare room or empty house was rented. The competition for housing led to general rent increases in Dragor, but these were slight for dwellings long in use.

In the postwar period, however, the situation altered radically. Houses are now very expensive to build. Small savings reservoirs no longer suffice even when combined with loans from relatives or friends, and the builder has to have money to pay for labor and materials. A new system of financing came into use, one which was well known to the capital but alien to the majority of the villagers—bank loans and mortgages. For most Dragorians, however, supplementary bank financing for independent home construction is prohibitive in cost, so building entrepreneurs in Copenhagen provide them with a different type of housing in the form of apartments or row houses. Through mass construction, the average wage earner can afford to buy an apartment or a part of a building.

For the upkeep of buildings and grounds, however, some form

of regularized supervision is necessary. This has been accomplished by the formation of cooperative associations, to which all co-owners of a single building belong. The association foreman is appointed by the contractor, and receives remuneration in the form of reduced rent. Complaints of serious proportions are dealt with through special meetings of the resident owners, but otherwise the foreman supervises property maintenance as well as the use of such common facilities as the basement laundries and drying rooms. The inhabitants of these new housing developments are both the young people of Dragor who need places for their new families and immigrant working families from Copenhagen. But whereas new units provide a place to live, payment for them consumes a greater proportion of the family earnings than had ever been the case in Dragor's history, and rent and mortgage payments are a very significant item of the family budget.

As more and more people moved to Dragor and as building rapidly increased, villa owners found that they shared common problems. They were concerned with such things as the placement of new roads, of underground pipes and electricity lines, and even the location of garbage dumps. For their mutual protection, they formed, during the 1940's, the land-owner society (*grundejerforening*) with a set of rules and a leadership of president, treasurer, and representatives. Officers meet periodically with the communal council to press the interests they represent. Members pay a yearly fee, but meetings are held only when there is a problem of consequence to be discussed.

Gone too are the days when water was free, lighting and fuel expenses minimal. Dragorians early felt the need for conveniences known to Copenhageners. In 1906 the communal government backed the establishment of a water and gas plant, and from 1915 to 1950 acted also as distributor of electricity. Dragor's water is today tapped from an underground source just north of the settlement. Gas is obtained by baking coal in the ovens of the gas and water works, and coke—a by-product of its production—provides present-day Dragorians with a cheaper fuel than they were otherwise able to purchase. Since the second world war central-heating units have been built into new dwellings and added to many of the old. Oil has also come to be used as fuel, though less popularly.

At first only the well-to-do could afford gas, electricity, and running water, but by the 1920's electricity was to be found in almost every home, and between the two world wars nearly all had gas and water installed. These regular expenses, however, once again allocated greater strains to the budget than was formerly the case for these needs.

The case is similar with sewage disposal, for the laying of sewer pipes in 1915 permitted the wealthier to install flush toilets and sink drains. The refuse middens were removed, and all garbage now has to be dumped in a single midden south of the town. In the same year a contract was issued to a wagoner to make regular pick-ups of garbage. Those not having toilets arranged to have their privy buckets emptied weekly by a special night pick-up. Flush toilets became more and more common, but in 1956 were still expensive to install, partly because sanitary laws prohibited their installation except by an authorized plumber and subject to inspection by a representative of the national department of sanitation. As a consequence, many of the old houses in Dragor still do not have water toilets, although all have sink drains. In 1957 the communal council passed an ordinance which requires that all houses have flush toilets by 1967, and it is expected that easy financing will be provided for those who otherwise can not afford the change. In any case, waste disposal has now become another regular expense for Dragorians.

Not the least significant motivation in the trend to a full money economy is the new-felt need for variety and for nonessential budget additions. It is now important, especially for young people, to have larger wardrobes, to own bicycles, motorbikes, or even automobiles, to have radios, and, since 1955, television. Refrigerators became popular after World War II, and now the small gas burners are being replaced by larger stoves with ovens. In order to be content, it is now necessary for most Dragorians to have money for all of these things, and lives are today geared to their acquisition.

8: The High Points in Life

The Yearly Round

IN old Dragor, feasts and ceremonies were crests in the flow of the year's work. They marked the termination of one period and the commencement of the next, and therefore were felt to be significant moments when many things were to be done. As in Viking times of old, the annual cycle of holidays fell into two periods, the longer period of midwinter and the shorter one of midsummer. Midwinter festivities began with the biggest celebration of them all, the Christmas–New Year's holidays, and ended with the second biggest, Shrovetide. The midsummer St. John's Day celebration brought the villagers to the next high point in the year, and even though it was a short-lived time of amusement, festivities were held with great enthusiasm. Only slight attention, on the contrary, was given to the spring holidays, Easter and Pentecost, and to the fall holiday, Harvest Sunday.

The Midwinter Fetes

For youngsters, at least, the Christmas season was launched the first week of December with the cry of a hired boy announcing, "Christmas display at Marchen Vester's." In the house of the old woman named Marchen Vester one room served as a shop where, throughout the year, she sold sugar confections (*brødsukker*), the product of her own humble kitchen. In early December, however, this simple inventory gave way suddenly to an enchanting exhibition of small toys fetchingly perched on shelves against two walls of the room. Until Christmas Eve the children came, again and again, opening the outside gate, wading through the yardful of geese, and timidly entering the shop to observe and discuss the item of doll furniture, the wooden soldier, or the toy carriage which had captured interest.

December days passed and the approaching festivities craved increasing thought and activity. One had to plan to be assured of a Yule with all the trimmings, and for the busy housewife the joy of preparation was somewhat thinned by the frenetic hustle and bustle it entailed. Regular household chores were scheduled so that everything would be clean and polished in time. By the middle of the month wreaths and sprays of evergreen and lichen decorated windows and doors, and a sheaf of wheat was hung for the birds on a tree or fence pole outside the house. The aroma from the small baking oven filled the house more and more frequently. Finally, a few days before Christmas, every housewife who could afford it put a large smoked ham in a pot of water to boil. *Paasegrød,* barley cooked in a bag, spiced with raisins, a bit of onion, and thyme, was boiled with the ham to profit from the smoked flavor.

For weeks the thrill of anticipation activated daily life and permeated conversation. Fruition began with "Little Christmas Eve" (*lille juleaften*) on the twenty-third of December. At noon of that day the hot meal was especially sumptuous; for many people it was the *paasegrød* sprinkled with honey-cake crumbs and served on a large platter so placed in the middle of the table that the whole family could spoon the barley directly from platter to mouth—side plates being used only for bits off the end of ham and leftovers. The ham itself would form the basis for a number of meals during the next couple of weeks. The rest of the day was devoted to preparing decorations for the Christmas tree.

Undoubtedly the biggest single day of the year was Christmas Eve (*Juleaften*). After a large meal in the evening, the family with their nearest relatives waited in hushed expectancy before the closed parlor door that was soon to reveal the Christmas tree. The tree was unveiled in the full glow of lighted candles, and the group joined hands to dance and sing around it. At last, when faces were glowing with the activity, the company settled down to exchange their presents and indulge in coffee and cakes.

In the weeks before the twenty-fourth, three or four poor old ladies had canvassed the village, selling a kind of small cookie (*pebbernødder*) to each household. On Christmas Eve each child

oking north on Strandstræde. These houses ed to be inhabited mainly by seamen and hermen. The cobbling of all the lanes in e village is a modern improvement.

Most streets open onto the Sound, admitting freezing blasts of wind in the winter. Nonetheless, the nursery-school children follow the footsteps of their ancestors in a daily walk.

e settlement is a mixture of old and new. is small *Irma* supermarket is just across the eet from an old-fashioned grocery shop on *ongevejen,* the favorite locale of modern ops.

As of old, the harbor grounds are reserved to the fishermen for the drying of nets. The building and tower in the background belong to the Royal Pilots.

A skipper's house in old Dragor. Indoor plumbing now makes the pump purely decorative. Straw roofs are still common.

The harbor is still the focal point of the village and fishermen have exclusive use of the quay nearest the viewer.

To the southwest in Meadow Park, middle-class and working-class families find a welcome haven from the crowded conditions of Copenhagen where they work.

Nineteenth-century *Holm's,* headquarters for the élite Skipper Society, is now the unobtrusive working man's restaurant at the end of the street.

and interested adult was given ten *pebbernødder* to be used in playing a game called *"Kis."* Each player contributed three or four of his cookies to a common pile in the center of the table. One player was selected to cover his eyes while a particular cookie chosen silently and at random by the other players was designated as "kis." The player then opened his eyes and withdrew cookies from the center pile one at a time, until the designated one was touched, at which everyone hilariously shouted "kis." The object was to get as many cookies as possible before being stopped and replaced in turn by the next player. The game was enlivened by adding a single hazelnut, which, though valued at ten *pebbernødder,* might also be designated "kis," making one hesitate to reach immediately for it.

The twenty-fifth of December, called "First Christmas Day" (*første juledag*), was a quiet day when activities were neither irreverently jovial nor boisterous, but centered on the afternoon church service. Second Christmas Day (*anden juledag*), December 26, on the contrary, was a joyous day devoted to exchanging visits with relatives or perhaps attending a ball.

The biggest balls of the year were sponsored during the midwinter holiday season by the two social clubs of the village, Unity and Skippers' Society. The membership of Skippers' Society comprised most shipmasters, ships' officers, and Sound pilots. Men of less esteemed occupations, excluded from membership with the village elite, belonged to Unity. Annually one society gave a Christmas ball and the other a New Year's ball, reversing the order every year. Since most family heads belonged to one of the two groups, those Dragorians not celebrating a Christmas party on the twenty-sixth of December attended a New Year's party on the thirty-first. It was extremely rare for one person to attend both functions in any one year, but the nature of the entertainment was virtually identical for the two balls, giving most villagers the diversion of a gala midwinter fête. In the prescribed sequence, each society also held an afternoon party for members' children, the adult activities beginning later in the evening.

The ball followed traditional patterns. Wearing their finest city clothes, the participants danced until three or four in the morning to the music of a small horn band. Each time the music started the men crossed the room to select a partner for a polka, mazurka, or quadrille. As is common in folk dancing, each person danced

with many partners before the night was out, and between turns
the men refreshed themselves at a large tureen of rum punch,
while the women more sedately nibbled at bits of fruit. Late
in the evening a long table was set up where coffee and cake were
served in shifts, since it was not possible to accommodate the
whole company at a single sitting.

On the twenty-eighth of December a tendency toward normal
was noted; stores were open again. But the yuletide spirit lived
on as residents visited friends and relatives to admire each other's
decorations, foods, and gifts, renewed energy expended in the
preceding days, and planned for a New Year's celebration soon
to come. That a minimal amount of work was done is hardly surprising, since this was an inactive season for virtually every occupation. Fishermen only occasionally tried to fish through the
winter ice; sailors, ships' officers, and pilots were equally harbor-
bound. Farmers had only minor routine chores, bleaching was
impossible, craftsmen were hindered in their work. Other business, and work not directly affected by the weather, was indirectly
slowed by the inability or unwillingness of the majority of the
citizens to pay for other than the most essential goods and services.

New Year's Eve was the only occasion in the year other than
Christmas Eve when most people had their hot meal in the evening, and the main course was preferably boiled salted eel with
mustard sauce. Many were up until midnight to guard against
youthful tricksters, but it was not traditional to greet the New
Year. Children threw flowerpots at house doors, the explosive
crashes rivaling the noise and fire of fireworks called "Chinamen"
(*kineser*) set off by older youths and family groups. Teenage
boys were also busy with even greater mischief, and the unwary
villager risked losing a fence gate or finding a barrel atop his
flagpole. In the harbor, life-sized dummies were attached to swing
from the riggings of icebound ships like so many executed pirates,
and many small boats, beached for the winter, ended up in the
front yard of the owner or on his roof. The single harassed
policeman had his busiest night of the year, rounding up offenders
who were locked for the night in the one-room jail called the
"dark hole" (*brummen*). Regarded as minor heroes by their
contemporaries and with indulgence by their elders, the young
transgressors considered the next week's trip by wagon to the

court in Copenhagen a lark well worth the fine they were sure
to receive.

Before going to bed on New Year's Eve, small children placed
a wooden shoe filled with apples in a window for *askefis*. No child
could be told what *askefis* looked like for no one had ever seen
him, but his existence was evidenced by the marzipan figure which
he left in the shoe after he had taken his food gifts. Its presence
the next morning promised a good new year. The child who did
not prepare a wooden shoe or would not sleep quietly on New
Year's Eve was sure to have ashes sprinkled in his eyes by the
fairy visitor.

On New Year's Day old ladies and children of poor families
went to the homes of the more prosperous to wish "Happy New
Year" (*glædelig nytaar*) receiving into a large apron the traditional gift of a Christmas bun (*julebol*). Since as many as three
or four members of a single family might make the rounds, a
goodly supply of these wheat loaves could be accumulated, repre-
senting a significant economic windfall for many winter-destitute
homes.

Beyond the poor element of the population, New Year's Day
was active only for the members of the association which had not
held a Christmas ball, for now it was their turn to enjoy the large
candle-lit tree and dance as the other group had done six days
before.

After the first of January the holiday spirit ebbed. There might
be still another meal on the Christmas ham. Cookies, nuts, and
candies would last a while yet, but the thrill now was in remem-
brance rather than in anticipation. The end came on January the
sixth, the day of the "Three Holy Kings" (*hellige tre konge*),
when the Christmas tree was taken out of the house and, in many
homes, three candles were lit on the evening coffee table. Such
was the simple, quiet ending of Yule.

The end of the winter season was marked by Shrovetide. Adult
Dragorians attended the masked ball of the society to which they
belonged. Both the Skippers' Society and the Unity ball were held
on Shrovetide Sunday, for this was the one holiday when dancing
was scheduled for the holiday proper.

The whole week before Shrovetide was active for the workers
who did not belong to one of the two associations. First, various

groups held a *læggelag,* when rum punch enlivened the planning of a private masquerade for their circle of friends and relatives, and the prospective participants pledged to share expenses. The Saturday-night ball in a rented hall or barn was much like the other adult parties except that the dances were more often polkas and mazurkas than quadrilles. In addition, the evening in the subsequent week when the men got together to split the costs provided another occasion for rummy joviality and the recitation of amusing anecdotes about the ball.

But if Shrovetide Sunday ended late with a lively ball for most adults, it began early when children awakened their parents by tickling and striking them with a *fastelavnris,* a cluster of small branches gaily decorated with figures, flowers, and bows of colored paper. During the day the streets were busy with small groups of costumed children knocking on doors, rattling boxes of coins and singing jingles appropriate to the holiday.

Others not thus occupied were running in flocks from one house to the next armed with wooden clubs for "striking the barrel" (*slaa til tønden*). For, in preceding days, small barrels had been painted with bright colors and fanciful designs until they were works of art—only to be sacrificed to the battering of excited children. The lucky one who finally knocked the bottom out of the barrel had a red ribbon placed on his arm and was designated the "barrel king."

On the two Mondays following Shrovetide Sunday, events occurred which would make conversation for the rest of the year: the visits of the farmers from Store Magleby. Impressive on their horses, the well-to-do Dutch-Danish farmers wore white silk shirts, embroidered vests with silver buttons and gold watchchain, riding pants and boots, and high black silk hats with gaily colored hat banding into which a small sheaf of wheat was tucked—made of silver on the first Monday when the riders were bachelors, of gold on the second when they were married men. As fancy as their masters, the horses had red ribbons braided into mane and tail. A flower arrangement on the crown of the animal's head covered a wooden block designed to protect should the rider—perhaps somewhat tipsy—miss the target and strike the horse instead when the time came for the barrel striking. Bridle trappings were decorated with hundreds of small shells sewn to the harnesses and hanging in rosettes, half-moons, and crosses. This shell decoration was first introduced into Denmark in 1677 by Croatian and Hungarian mercenaries. In the middle of the nineteenth century, specimens were purchased from the regimental saddle maker by the local farmers who had become acquainted with the decoration as army conscripts.

Each year the twenty or thirty Store Magleby riders visited the farms and inns of their home village and of Dragor. At each stop they dismounted to approach a large bowl of rum punch and to drink a toast to the farmer or innkeeper and his family, eat apple cakes and dance a polka or two with the women spectators to the music of the small horn band that accompanied the procession. In Dragor they were followed by the whole town eager to watch, the girls hoping for a dance, the men, for a glass of punch—all impressed with the pageantry, feverishly enthused by high riders on skittish horses clattering through narrow cobblestone streets, wheeling sharply into line before the honored host.

At four in the afternoon of these two Mondays, Dragor resembled a ghost town, everyone having walked to "Dutchtown" to watch the riders "strike the barrel." Originally called "knocking the cat out of the barrel'" (*slaa katten af tønden*), the mounted participants had not so mistreated a live cat since 1733, at which time they also ceased the Shrovetide tradition of "pulling the head off the goose" (*trække halsen af gaasen*). This latter sport, a diversion shared by the local Dutch with the merchants of Bergen, Norway, required the equestrian to yank at the soap-slippery neck of a suspended goose while riding at a full gallop. The rider who completed the decapitation was the winner. But if in 1890 celebrants were less barbaric than formerly, it was still a colorful time. The barrel was painted in red and blue, the Dutch national colors, and the hoops were painted silver for the bachelors, gold for the benedicts.

The barrel king, red band of victory on his sleeve, danced the first three dances at the ball that evening in Store Magleby Inn with the barrel queen, always the oldest unmarried girl of their village. Since the only Dragorians welcome at the farmers' ball were the two farmers who were their relatives, the remainder of the day's colorful events in Store Magleby now withdrew behind a kinship barrier, leaving Dragorians to their own devices. Returning to their village, the latter sought diversion in the spontaneous, though predictable dance at the Old Inn, the one time of the year when women entered its cellar room. Girls, the daughters of fishermen, sailors, and workers, managed to find themselves near enough to the inn to be attracted by the music of an accordion to dance until midnight in a room darkly lit by flickering petroleum lamps. Paying nothing and served nothing, they had as much fun as the young men, who, beer steins in hand, did not let a lass rest for long on the bench along the wall.

The Midsummer Fete

The Eve of St. John (*St. Hansaften*) on the twenty-third of June was significant for the three farmers in the village, for on this day the first potatoes were traditionally harvested to be sold in Copenhagen. For the village as a whole it was a festival day. The association that was known as "Dragor's Future" sponsored a carnival in the park in which the villagers had cooperated to set up amusement stands offering prizes in games of chance or skill. In the early evening of this, the longest day of the year, bonfires were lit along the beach. Lateral to a big fire, a score of smaller ones, often kindled by young boys, attracted groups of people to chat while watching across the Sound for fires burning on the Swedish beach and warming hands at their own against the cool evening breeze. Finally, the still bright midnight hours witnessed the year's one all-village dance. Held in the open park and attended by every social segment, it was the summer's gay but short-lived rival to the social activities of the winter months.

Spring and Fall Fetes

Easter loomed large on the church calendar. Holy Thursday (*skærtorsday*) and Good Friday (*Langfredag*) were solemn days when all places of business were closed. Easter Sunday (*paaske*) was a peaceful family holiday (*stille og rolige familie fest*), seriously regarded because of its religious significance. A holiday dinner was served, traditionally a kale stew (*grønlangkaal*), but normally few guests were invited. Second Easter Day (*anden paaskeday*) was equally quiet. The sole enlivenment of these days occurred when the children went to the town park to throw and roll Easter eggs on the grass.

On Pentecost (*pinse*), according to a local proverb, "one must get out of bed early to see the sun dance." Many, indeed, were up early to see the sun rise and to take a brisk walk along the beach. The whole village later congregated at the church, for this was a holiday in which it was traditionally obligatory to go to mass in order to "attend the offering." Otherwise there was little to distinguish Pentecost from an ordinary, quiet Sunday.

The sole fall fete was Harvest Sunday, marked only by a sermon of thanksgiving by the priest and the decoration of the church with fall leaves and flowers.

The Modern Cycle of Holidays

The midsummer, fall, and spring fetes, always less distinctive than those of the midwinter schedule when the men were all home, survive relatively unchanged from the nineteenth century.

Between 1910 and 1935, however, the winter holidays lost most of their local distinctiveness and came to be indistinguishable from practices in Copenhagen. Today, in Dragor, these holidays no longer occasion the eating of *paasegrød* for Christmas or of boiled eel on New Year's Eve. *Kis* is not played on Christmas Eve and poor people do not beg buns on New Year's Day. On New Year's Eve most people stay indoors to listen to the nationally broadcast radio program, and youthful pranks are kept to a minimum by an alert force of uniformed, mechanized police. Nor do children leave a wooden shoe for *askefis* on this evening. In fact, few of them now own wooden shoes. At Shrovetide the special *"strutter"* buns are no longer eaten, and barrels are only sporadically painted and broken.

The most significant loss, however, occurred just before or during World War I when the balls of the societies ceased to be a major diversion of village life. The Unity Society disbanded about 1910, and the Skippers' Society was then attracting only a few of the older merchant-officer families. Public commercial dances took the place of the old, intimate balls and appealed only to a portion of the young people. With the disappearance of the balls vanished much of the stimulating local cohesiveness in holiday celebrations and their distinctive local color as well.

Holidays in modern Dragor are typified by the retention of the generalized Danish substratum of traditions characteristic of city life. Almost the only distinctive survival of local custom is the continued riding of the Dutch farmers at Shrovetide, a practice which seems well on the road to extinction.

But the generalized Danish customs have themselves changed

greatly since the 1930's. This change may be characterized as the product of a marked development of commercialism. Christmas decorations and presents, Shrovetide branches, even Easter eggs are now purchased in stores rather than made in the homes. The emphasis at Christmas, especially, has shifted from the pleasures of an intimate family holiday to the exchange of valuable presents.

With the decreasing emphasis on local traditions and the mounting spirit of commercialism have developed concomitant tendencies on the part of adults to enjoy the holidays primarily because they are not work days, and to restrict social participation in residual traditions to home celebration with members of the domestic family or to commercial halls and restaurants with friends. The former division of the festive year into a great midwinter celebration and a lesser midsummer one has been modified into virtual extinction. Only the fete days themselves are workfree in the winter, and in the summer one works on St. John's Day. To this local-level adjustment has been added the establishment by law of a number of national holidays which are compulsory days of rest. The total effect on the annual Dragorian cycle has been a radical change from a schedule of seasonal high points to a more or less even spacing of work-free days throughout the year.

Rites of Passage

In addition to the annual cycle of holidays, the yearly roster of special events in old Dragor included rites of passage. These special, distinctly religious ceremonies, were, like the holidays, high points of the year, providing a break in the day-to-day activities of the village and the memory highlights of a lifetime. Their occurrence, of course, is timed by individual life rhythms rather than by the calendar as such.

Baptism

In the intimacy of village life everyone knew where a baby was expected and when a birth had occurred. Other than in neighborly gossip, however, no public notice was taken of an arrival until the baptismal ceremony.

On the Sunday before the scheduled baptism the mother, called *kirkegangskone* (literally, the "going-to-church-woman"), attended church. It was the first time since the birth a couple of weeks to two months before that she had been permitted to leave the house. The priest said a special prayer, and blessed her.

All near relatives and close friends and neighbors were invited to the rite. The greater the number of guests, the greater the prestige of the parents, for it demonstrated ability to entertain and largely determined the amount of money offered at the two church tables. Poor families were often inclined to invite large gatherings, including well-to-do neighbors, but failed to advance in prestige since they could only afford to serve coffee and cake afterwards.

During the ceremony the child was held by the "woman sponsor" (konefadder). A "girl sponsor" (pigefadder) held the hat of the infant while the priest sprinkled its head. The "man sponsor" (mandefadder) had no duties and was frequently not even present, but off somewhere at sea. The sponsors were always relatives of the parents. The girl sponsor had to be unmarried and was most commonly a sister of one of the parents. That her role was minor was reflected in the fact that her name did not appear in the church records. The woman sponsor was generally the paternal or maternal grandmother of the infant, or a sister of a grandparent. Ill will might occur in her selection since it was regarded as an honor and, in addition to closeness of kinship, the criteria of selection included how highly the relative was regarded by the community, especially in terms of wealth. A woman not selected might well be offended as not having been considered good enough. The man sponsor was usually the husband of the woman sponsor. In addition to the vaguely defined requirement that they be responsible for the Christian education of the child should the parents "fall away," the adult sponsors were supposed to give a small, silver gift to the infant, commonly a spoon or a rattle. When the child learned to speak he used appropriate kinship terms in addressing his baptismal sponsor, the fact of godparenthood remaining only a dim memory.

When, at the designated moment in the ritual, the priest asked for the name of the child, it was given him by the woman sponsor. Until that moment a secret known only to parents and godmother, it had been selected perhaps with considerable difficulty, for while it was the custom to name the child after a close relative, there were alternatives, and hard feelings might develop as a result of the choice. Generally the first child was named after the father's father, a girl getting a version with a feminine ending such as *Hansine* for *Hans, Jacobine* for *Jacob,* or *Carline* for *Carl.* If the second child were a boy it would be named after the mother's father. If it were a girl, the mother's father's name (in feminine version), father's mother's, or mother's mother's would be equally suitable. The rule, thus only vaguely defined, was further subject to considerations of prestige, which might give preference to the maternal grandparents.

The ritual over, the members of the baptismal party filed towards the altar to lay money on the offering tables. An additional two-crown piece was given the priest by the woman sponsor if the baptized were a boy, by the girl sponsor if a girl. The party then adjourned to the home of the parent where a celebration was held.

Coffee and an array of special pastries and cakes were first served, and in order to accommodate all of the guests at a sitting it was often necessary to build a temporary table of long boards. By the time coffee was finished it was late afternoon. The men who were present walked to the locale of the association to which they belonged to spend an hour or two playing cards and sipping rum toddies, while the women remained to discuss infant care, being treated, after a bit, to a serving of preserved fruit. All ate from a large common bowl. Since most households owned no more than one or two spoons fine enough for the occasion, it was customary for each guest to use the same spoon in turn, placing it in a glass of water after a mouthful was taken, to be picked up by the adjoining guest. In the homes of the better-off, the men returned at six or six-thirty to join the women at the dinner table where kale (*grønlangkaal*) and ham were usually served. The spirit was gay but reserved, for this was regarded as a ceremonious (*højtidlig*) occasion.

On the following Sunday, the parents and sponsors attended mass and went forward together to partake of communion.

In contemporary Dragor baptism continues to mark the first public attention given an infant, and the rite itself remains essentially unchanged. Certain former observances related to baptism, however, are considerably altered or have disappeared. During World War I it ceased to be the custom for the mother to be confined to her home until just before the ceremony, and with this practice went the already attenuated churching rite.

Guests are restricted to a small number of the closest relatives and one or two close friends. During the ceremony the child may be held by the mother or father, godmother or godfather. Rarely is there a girl sponsor to occupy herself with the infant's hat, nor is it now even considered fashionable for the infant to wear a hat.

Church rules now require that four sponsors (two male and two female) be entered into the church books. The selection of these sponsors is very casual. Often two of them are the parents themselves. Some people pick an employer or an influential acquaintance, but this is not common. Most frequently, the sponsors are of the same age as the parents, either personal friends, siblings, or close relatives. The age factor is cited as related to the disadvantage of having a sponsor who might be too advanced in years, or dead at the time he or she could be called upon to perform the duty of parent-surrogate with respect to Christian education—an unconvincing argument since the sponsors are rarely thought of once the ritual is over and their names are entered into the church books. A gift from the sponsor to the infant is still customary. Today it is often a few crowns in a bank account. One of the women sponsors is still considered the most important, and since approximately 1915 she has been called *gudmor* (godmother) rather than *konefadder,* conforming to contemporary Copenhagen usage. If her husband is one of the male sponsors he will be called *gudfar* (godfather) but in cases where the sponsors are not married couples there need not be a godfather especially designated.

When the priest asks for the name of the child it is given by the mother or the godmother, whichever is holding the child. The name is still not made public until this moment. Children are sometimes named after relatives, but the grandfather is not particularly favored and the name of the parents is rarely given. Most commonly, however, the child is given a name chosen for its esthetic appeal. This custom, superseding the old, quite prescribed system of nomenclature, developed in the second decade of this century and since that period distinct fads in name giving have been evident. In 1945 American names were popular; in 1957 the trend was prevalently to Italian names. Throughout this century a number of Dragorian children have been given old local names, especially those of Dutch origin. This has been true of recent immigrants as well as of indigenous families, all of whom feel that the names have the advantage of distinctiveness and are esthetically pleasing.

The offering tables were removed from the church in 1910 when the new town constitution was adopted.

The postbaptismal festivities are restricted for the most part to coffee and cake in the afternoon. In the few cases where dinner is served to the guests, numbers rarely exceed fifteen. Men now remain throughout the day with the rest of the party. Eating of preserved fruit is no longer a special custom. The use of a communal silver spoon began to disappear at the turn of the century, and by 1920 was found only among a few old Dragorian families.

The most striking change of all, however, is the lost universality of the baptismal rite. Whereas formerly every child had to be baptized in order for its birth to be recorded, it is now possible to forego the religious ceremony and have the birth registered civilly. Although only a relatively small number of contemporary Dragorians do not baptize their children, those not baptizing defy tradition in this manner without encountering public reproval.

Confirmation

In the 1890's the children of poor Dragorians started planning for their confirmation years before the actual ceremony. From the time they got their first part-time jobs, which might be as early as age seven or eight, they saved money for the purchase of clothes. Proper clothes and money for other expenses were so important for the young individual that there was even a charitable organization, "The Cork Society," which had as its sole purpose the giving of financial help to needy confirmation celebrants.

The fourteenth birthday was the signal for participation in the next scheduled rite, which was preceded by six months of special Friday-afternoon catechism classes conducted by the local pastor. Confirmation was held twice a year, on a Sunday in spring and in the fall.

The girls wore long black dresses with black gloves, their pigtails tied in a bun on the back of the neck, unadorned by hat or veil. In the hand was carried a new missal (*psalmebog*) and a white lace handkerchief. Boys wore a new dark-blue suit which would serve as Sunday best until worn out or outgrown, sometimes never replaced until, ten or more years later, they purchased a new suit for their wedding. The boys, too, carried a missal.

Before the ceremony, in the church itself, in front of the assembled families and relatives, each aspirant was examined orally by the priest, a test which no child had ever failed.

The key act in the confirmation ritual came when the priest asked each boy or girl, "Dost thou renounce the devil and all his works and kingdom? Dost thou believe in God the Father, in Jesus Christ, his only begotten Son and in the Holy Spirit, as our Christian belief dictates? Is it thy desire to remain in this, thy baptismal pact, until thy last hour?" After the inevitable affirmative reply, the priest blessed the aspirants in turn and the ritual was ended.

During the afternoon a dinner party was held for the closest relatives, after which the celebrants, still wearing their confirmation suits and dresses, walked about the village giving small coins to their schoolmates.

Sunday passed and Monday came, the time for all members of the confirmation class to don their "second-day clothes" and visit the pastor's home. No special clothing was prescribed for the boys, but "second-day clothes" for the girls consisted of a party skirt with a flowered blouse after the adult style. At the pastor's home, hot chocolate and cakes were served. On adjourning from the dining room to the sitting room, each participant left a fancy envelope containing a money gift—ten crowns from the well-to-do, five from most families, less from the poor. The subsequent humor of the priest was said to depend on how much money he got, for he had an opportunity hurriedly to count the collection before joining the others, who were chatting, self-consciously gay.

Tuesday or Wednesday evening, wearing "second-day clothes" again, the initiates attended a special communion service (*altergang*), the first time they were permitted to partake of the sacrament. Almost without exception, the communicant was accompanied by one or both parents at this sacred rite and for the rest of that day anyone meeting either youth or parent said, "congratulations and blessings" (*til lykke og velsignelse*) according to local practice.

On the evening following the first communion, the school

teacher traditionally invited the communicants for coffee. This party, the last of the festivities associated with confirmation, was for most boys and girls the last prescribed meeting with their teacher, and universal high spirits made it clear that confirmation meant less as a religious act than as the signal for the termination of school attendance and the assumption of adult activities.

Confirmation today is still a very big event socially in the life of a Dragorian. The minor role of its purely religious content, however, has become increasingly apparent. In 1956 when one group of candidates for confirmation was asked by the priest if they believed in God, over one half answered that they did not, and of the remaining pupils, one half again answered that they were unsure. They were confirmed, nevertheless, on the grounds that they were really too young to have a proper understanding of Christian belief. Only half of the confirmants, many of them unaccompanied by their parents, attend the first communion service.

Practices that formerly distinguished Dragorians from Copenhageners disappeared by the second decade of the new century. This includes the parties given by the pastor and the teacher, the distribution of small coins by the confirmants, and the village benediction *"til lykke og velsignelse."*

Boys dress, as of old, in blue suits and ties whose style has changed but superficially in the intervening years. Girls now wear white dresses rather than black. The change first occurred in 1904 when two girls of well-to-do families got permission to follow the custom already popular in Copenhagen. In 1905 other girls followed suit and by 1906 all girls wore white. There is some pressure on the part of the priest and some parents to inaugurate the use of robes which would be owned by the church and rented at a nominal sum by the candidates. Their aim is to put an end to competitive dressing, and would end the difficulty of so many parents who invest more than they can afford for clothes.

The focus of confirmation interest has become the party, which, since 1920 has steadily grown bigger and most festive. In addition to nearest family members, many friends of the parents and the candidates are invited. Since the party may be held within a period of several weeks after the ritual and since many churches throughout greater Copenhagen schedule their services for the same season many young people attend one another's parties.

The party was no longer felt to be necessarily solemn, and

dancing and drinking were added to the festive dinner. Many rented a party hall in one of the public inns. Gifts too became more extravagant, especially on the part of nearer relatives.

The expense of putting on such a party was sometimes a determining factor in postponing the ritual itself until the child was sixteen, and many a parent went into debt to manage it. As a result, there has been within the last ten years evidence of a tendency to alter the custom, limiting the size and scope of the party or substituting for it a larger gift to the confirmant, such as a motorbike or a trip abroad.

Since the 1930's a small number of people have undergone the so-called civil confirmation (*borgerlig confirmation*) rather than the church rite. This ceremony is studiously nonreligious, conducted in Copenhagen by governmental authorities. Stress is laid on the fact that the young person is entering a turning point in his life and should make every effort to be an honest, hardworking, patriotic citizen. Although this development reflects a decrease in the influence of Christian belief, Dragorian youngsters, almost without exception, seek out some type of confirmation rite with the conventional church service predominantly favored.

Marriage

In the 1890's, the girl who married a young fisherman from a poor family could expect only a very simple celebration. Banns would be announced for three Sundays by the priest and the wedding would occur in church, but only close relatives and friends would be invited. The number was kept between ten and twenty. In the afternoon after the church rites, the wedding party had a roast-pork dinner at the home of the bride. No musicians, no dancing, and few speeches enlivened the gathering. The party broke up at midnight and the newlyweds were free to retire to the small apartment or house that would be their home.

Weddings of the better-off were quite another thing. Some weeks in advance young girls within the bride's family, or the young domestic, "went around and invited" (*gik rundt og bi*) to two or three places each afternoon, reciting a standard invitation, such as "I am to greet you from Pilot-bookkeeper Palm and wife to ask if you will come to the wedding of their daughter Marchen and Shipmaster Taarnby, the sixteenth of October." (*Jeg skulde hilse fra Lodsbogholder Palm og frue om De ville komme til bryllup*

hos deres datter Marchen og Skibsfører Taarnby den 16. oktober.)
Most accepted the invitation, but if some could not they were
replaced by others until a full house of about one hundred guests
had been assured.

Only invited guests attended the church ceremony. Rings were
not exchanged, this having been done when the couple became
"ring-betrothed," and the short ritual, starting at four P.M. was
over by four-thirty. Dinner was served afterwards in a rented
banquet room—usually at Holm's. Porcelain, silverware, and tablecloths were borrowed for the occasion from relatives and friends,
the hired rooms having neither kitchen nor table equipment. For
the preparation and serving of the meal the bride's parents' siblings had been invited as "cooks," the men fetching the roasts from
the bakery where they were prepared and carving them while the
women added potatoes and gravy.

The dinner was festive. First, rice porridge was eaten, each man
and wife eating this course, but only this one, from a plate shared
between them. The meat dish was always a roast, and the dessert
was almond cake (*kransekage*). A sour red wine, to which sugar
was added, was considered proper to the main course, port wine
to the cake—wines having replaced beer as more fitting for the
then "modern" decade of the nineties. Glasses were raised frequently in toasts to the bridal couple, their parents, and more
honored guests. A four-man horn orchestra accompanied the
singing of songs, the words composed by a friend or relative and
printed with illustrative drawings. The unprinted melodies were
old and familiar.

After the long dinner, the musicians played, leading a procession out of the building and through the winding streets of the
village. The whole wedding party followed, regardless of the
weather. By the time they returned to the hall, it had been cleared
for dancing, with two tables set up for punch, one bearing a rum
punch for the men, another a mild red-wine punch for the ladies.
At least once during the evening, each man dropped a crown or
more into a bowl on the floor in front of the musicians to ensure
continued good music. The bridegroom and the fathers of the
couple made especially generous contributions. At eleven, a table
was set up where coffee and cake, and glasses of rum (for the
men), were served in shifts until all had eaten. Dancing continued.
At two A.M. kale stew (*grønlangskaal*) and beer in pewter-topped

steins fortified the celebrants who continued in high humor until five or six in the morning.

Festivities continued the next day with the "second day's wedding" (*anden dags bryllup*) held in the home of the bride's parents. Only the closest relatives were invited, and the dinner this time was served by the siblings of the bride and bridegroom. The last wedding event was the so-called "cooks' wedding" (*kokkebryllup*) when dinner followed by coffee was served for those who had acted as cooks on the first wedding day. This party always took place on the subsequent Thursday.

Today, although the essence of the church ritual remains unchanged, customs formerly associated with large weddings have been greatly altered and conform to standards set in the capital.

After approximately 1910 it ceased to be the custom in Dragor to "go around and invite," and written invitations instead came into use.

Not infrequently, all of those invited to the church are asked to a reception where coffee and cake are served, but then only a small number are invited to remain for dinner. The reception and dinner are usually held in the home of the bride, occasionally in the home of the bridegroom, and only rarely in a public place. In private homes the hostess is assisted in the preparation of food by hired help, by one of the large number of women in town who earn extra money by performing this service. There is thus no longer a "cooks' wedding" to repay the help of relatives in the kitchen. The march of the members of the wedding party and musicians through town has also ended, coincident with the lesser use of public halls which developed between 1910 and 1915. If the reception is held in a public place, the party is quite different from the nineties. Such a place now has its own porcelain and silver, cooks who prepare the food in the kitchen, and waiters to serve. The festivities themselves are simpler and rarely involve more than a small dinner party.

The "second wedding day" has also disappeared except in very attenuated form as an informal get-together of close relatives to consume the remains of the preceding day's food specialities.

Only one civil wedding was reported in Dragor for the last decade of the nineteenth century. In subsequent decades a growing incidence was observable until now they are as common as

religious ceremonies. Reasons vary for favoring the civil wedding rite, which is performed by the mayor in the council building, but the following arguments are most frequently cited: it is
quicker, cheaper, and executed with a minimum of attention and
fuss from relatives and friends. The custom of the honeymoon
trip has been introduced, and not infrequently the time and
money saved through a simple civil ceremony are invested in a
longer, more expensive excursion than would otherwise be possible.

Funeral

In the last decade of the nineteenth century when a Dragorian
died two or three girls, relatives or domestics of the deceased,
were sent out to "let it be known" (*lade vide*). Only those so
notified were invited to the funeral, and only the invited attended.
The form of the notification was always the same, "I am to greet
you from Peder Hendrik's wife and say that her husband is dead
and will be buried on Tuesday" (*Jeg skulde hilse fra Peder
Hendriks kone at hendes mand er død og skal begraves paa
tirsdag*). It was recited even though everyone already had heard
through indirect channels. A couple of days later the actual invitation was given, again by young girls, the so-called "request
children" (*bedebørn*). This invitation always took the form,
"We are to greet you from Peder Hendrik's wife (to ask) if you
will follow her husband to the last resting place on Tuesday at
two o'clock and go along home and drink coffee" (*Vi skulde
hilse fra Peder Hendriks kone om De vil følge hendes mand til
det sidste hvilested paa tirsdag klokken to og gaa med hjem og
drikke kaffe*). The invitation was extended to all relatives no
matter how remote, as well as to near friends.

People invited to the funeral also followed the hearse (*ligvogn*)
which, drawn by horses covered with black drapes, on the day
after the death removed the body from the house to the chapel.
Six male relatives in dark suits acted as pall bearers (*ligbærer*)
between house and carriage, carriage and chapel. In the chapel
the casket rested unopened and unvisited until the day of the
funeral.

When that day arrived the relatives and friends appeared at the
church wearing black. The funeral service included a procession
"to attend the offering" at the offering tables, followed by a

eulogy for the deceased. The body, resting in front of the altar and surrounded by flowers, was then carried to the cemetery (*kirkegaard*) beside the church where it was lowered into the grave. When the final prayer was said over the grave, the members of the funeral party walked solemnly to the home of the deceased where coffee and cakes were served. The closest relatives stayed on for a roast dinner and more coffee, leaving at nine or nine-thirty in the evening. Conversation was respectful but not morbid, and most people enjoyed the occasion to chat and have refreshments. One had an obligation, in fact, to make the occasion enjoyable.

Relatives went into "deep mourning" for six months and semimourning for three months if the deceased were a child, parent, parent's sibling, or grandparent. For near relatives other than these, the period of deep mourning lasted for one month from the day of the funeral with semimourning for another five months. "Deep mourning" for a spouse lasted at least one year, often two, and sometimes was continued for life. Old women were conspicuous for their black garments, since they were in mourning so often that usually they simply wore black as permanent dress, foregoing the expense of other clothes which they might not be able to wear very much.

For men mourning clothes were not a problem. They continued to wear working clothes during the week, and the suit of clothes worn on Sundays and to festivities was, with the addition of a black tie, very suitable. It had been different earlier in the century when men wore more colorful village dress, but in the nineties only older women wore the regional costume. For them, "deep mourning" meant in effect that the colorful shawls and aprons that adorned the every-day black dress were replaced by dark ones. "Semimourning" permitted a bit of color such as a black apron with small white polka dots. For weddings, confirmation, and baptisms when they would otherwise wear the colorful red "Amager-dress," they donned, during mourning periods, a special black version appropriate to formal occasions. The requirements of dress thus called for three versions of the national frock: an every-day black one, a fine black one for funeral and special events while in mourning, and a bright red one for festive occasions. Younger women and girls who wore "modern" dress, however outmoded it may have been regarded by the contemporary

Copenhageners, were subject to the same requirements as the old ladies with respect to mourning color.

Today the notification of death is unstylized by the employment of "asking girls." It is done by telephone, in personal visits, by letter or engraved announcement. An obituary notice, including a description of the qualities and achievements of the deceased, is published in one of the Copenhagen dailies where it may attract the attention of interested people not otherwise informed.

It is considered a display of friendliness and kindness to attend a funeral, even though not personally invited, and afterwards to shake hands with the members of the family of the deceased to express sympathy. Those attending the church service uninvited do not usually follow to the cemetery where a final prayer is said before the body is lowered in the grave. Old Dragorian families invite the nearest family and the closest friends at the graveside to come home with them to have a cup of coffee and cake. The priest is no longer automatically a member of such a party, and although he would not be unwelcome, he no longer attends unless specifically invited.

Since the 1930's women have ceased to follow the stringent rules for mourning and now wear black only for a few weeks for a husband, father, child, or sibling, and just for the day of the funeral for any other near relative. Until recently men wore a black band on the sleeves of suit jackets for periods varying from a month to six months, but within the last five years this too has ceased to be customary. A few compromise with a small black ribbon in the lapel, but most use no emblem at all. The last local women wearing the Amager costumes died or discarded the dress during the 1940's.

Retirement

In the second decade of the twentieth century, a new rite was introduced, principally for the men, between the wedding and the funeral. It has become an almost indispensable consideration to celebrate "the retirement party." An elaboration of the basic pattern for dinner parties and always including the presentation of a gift from the person's firm or fellow employees, the retirement party has no religious association but rivals the older rites of passage in magnificence and interest.

Summation

The rites of passage were not so directly affected by the yearly economic cycle as were the cyclical feasts and ceremonies. Funerals took place unpredictably and the time of confirmation was determined by the school program. Baptisms did tend to occur in the spring, since the midwinter season was the period when a high percentage of infants were conceived, and weddings were rare except between December and February when the men were in port. Baptisms and weddings now occur sporadically throughout the year.

Both the cyclical fetes and the rites of passage have become single-day observances. In this they are undoubtedly affected by economic changes. Midwinter is no longer a time of prevalent unemployment during which it is convenient to seek amusement.

In the nineties and today, celebrations appear to have the implicit function of reifying and solidifying social ties. Change has occurred, however, in the kinds of social relations which are thus reinforced. Kinship, neighborhood, communal propinquity, and class have weakened as bases for festive gatherings, leaving the ties of the domestic family and elective individual ties predominant. This is reflected even in the changes in name-giving procedure. The growing role of associations, moreover, is mirrored in an increase in voluntary association parties. It is now common to convene a membership for the express purpose of celebrating a holiday or to honor an individual on a special day in his life.

Although altered, the rites of passage and the annual holidays are still deeply entrenched in Dragorian life. Whatever losses of tradition the townspeople may have undergone, they still want celebrations that vary the otherwise monotonous weekly rhythm of six days of work and one day of rest. It also continues vital to be brought together in intimate social groups at special times, even though the nature of the group has changed. The rites of passage are tenacious. In the face of pronounced weakening of associated religious feelings, drama is nevertheless still incumbent in the changing of roles during the course of a lifetime.

9: The Social Structure [1]

CATEGORICALLY, the institutions that ordered society in the harbor village of the nineties and channeled the personal relations of its men, women, and children persist in the urban community of today. Structurally, however, they have altered, some profoundly, and exemplify varying adaptations to urban pressures. One finds a mounting dependency of the community as well as the individual on voluntary associations, which appears particularly when they are contrasted to family and kin, class, age grades, neighborhood, and church. It is a pre-eminence, however, which associations must share with another institution—the government. The growth of governmental agencies matches that of associations in increased complexity and range of influence.

Family and Kin

The importance of family and kin groups has declined in Dragør since 1890. For the early village population the nuclear family was generally an indispensable economic as well as a basic social unit. In fishing families all members gave regular assistance to the head of the family in cleaning, repairing, and constructing equipment. The daily preparation of hooks and traps was a fam-

[1] Substantial parts of this chapter have appeared in "Voluntary Associations and Urbanization: A Diachronic Analysis," *American Journal of Sociology*, LXV (November, 1959), 265–73, and in "Changing Social Stratification in a Danish Village," *Anthropological Quarterly*, XXXIII (April, 1960), 98–105. See also "The Timing Mechanism in Culture Lag Reduction: Changing Kinship in a Danish Community," *Kroeber Anthropological Society Papers* (Fall, 1958), 87–101.

ily enterprise, a son was commonly a sailing assistant to his father, and many wives peddled their husbands' catch.

Wives and children also constituted a regular part of the work force for the linen bleachers, farmers, storekeepers, innkeepers, and drayers.

A declining vitality is particularly evident today in kinship bonds formerly effective beyond the nuclear family, that is, the *nærmeste familie* and *slægtninger*. The former group congregated regularly to celebrate Christmas Eve, baptisms, confirmations, and weddings and to attend funerals. It consisted of husband, wife, children, spouses of married children plus anyone in a nuclear family relationship with any member of the core group. Exchanges of visits and mutual aid within it were common. *Slægtninger* included anyone with whom a consanguineal tie, however remote, was traceable, or the spouse of someone in such a relationship. *Slægtninger* met as a group at funerals and large weddings and thus had a real, though tenuous, social existence.

In modern Dragor, familial integrity is considerably lessened both as a social and as an economic force. The myriad joint-labor demands of the moribund fishing-maritime economy no longer exist, and for only a few, now, is solvency contingent upon family solidarity and singleness of effort. The strength of the family as a social unit has been weakened by the widespread daily dispersal of its members at work and by the decrease, often related, in parental authority. Whereas formerly it was common for the father to exercise absolute jurisdiction, with the mother second in command, now, typically, children assume increasing freedom with increasing age—culminating, often in adolescence, in behavior regarded by many adults as rebellious and disobedient. While some parents are less disparaging of the relaxation of standards, all are agreed that the internal structure of the family has altered. Divorce, unrecorded for the nineties, is now an intrusive problem.

The *nærmeste familie* and *slægtninger* are less distinct than formerly as observable groups. Christmas Eve and baptism have become events confined to the domestic family. The few friends and other relatives invited are almost all included solely on the basis of shared interest. Weddings, confirmations, and funerals remain the traditional occasions for the uniting of the *nærmeste familie*. The tendency, however, is to hold more intimate and unpretentious gatherings for the enjoyment of the nuclear family and select friends, attesting again to the lessened social importance of kin ties.

Class

Marine employment was highly regarded and other work held in invidious comparison. The hierarchy by which individuals were ranked in prestige by others of the community was based upon the hierarchy of command aboard ship, somewhat modified to incorporate the whole population. The resultant social divisions were correlated, as we shall see, with a stratified panvillage network of work-time and leisure-time groups, some formal and others informal in structure.

Almost without exception a man's prestige derived from the specific nature of his maritime employment. His wife and children were ranked accordingly. Three ranked groups evolved. The skippers, pilots, and ships' officers together formed the community's upper stratum. The bulk of the population—seamen, most fishermen, and skilled artisans—were grouped apart from and below that of the marine leadership, but above a virtually prestigeless group of unskilled laborers and those fishermen and seamen who had forfeited status, generally because of moral turpitude, chronic alcoholism, or an aversion to work.

These were the core reference groups. These were Dragor's classes. Against this distribution the remainder of the population was assessed and ranked in prestige. Not every dry-land occupation ranked low on the scale. In the equation between land-based and sea-based occupations, the tacit understanding seems to have been that, in spite of a less commendable type of work, the power and consequent social weight of certain personages negated their placement at a mean level.

Professions that required a formal education and which placed a person in a position of leadership, such as priest and the head school teacher were equated on a level that approached that of the skippers and pilots and ships' officers and was sufficiently above that of seamen and fishermen to be placed with the former. The three farmers were envied their wealth but not their work, but their advantage in capital goods placed them in the upper stratum, despite their occupation. Master craftsmen ranked just below ships' officers, and journeymen were considered on a plane with seamen and fishermen.

Dragorians themselves recognized "fine people" (the upper class), "ordinary people" (the middle), and "poor people" (the lower).

It is significant that in the nineteenth-century village these groups had corporate existence. Dragor's classes were discernible and fixed in their loci, and the activity of their membership was socially prescribed and predictable. There was little class mobility.

In the frozen midwinter months when ice closed the harbor, most mariners were port-bound. For seamen and their families time passed in sedentary tasks; the fishermen mended nets and repaired equipment, and the village celebrated its biggest holidays while the men were home. During this period of maximum socializing the grouping of classes is most discernible.

Every day at three-thirty or four P.M. weather permitting, seamen gathered to tour the harbor, to observe and discuss wind and ships. A year-round routine, it was enhanced by the number of men in port at this time. They formed a number of groups, the membership of which was prescribed. Each group confined itself to a specific area. Shipmasters gathered by the harbor office, ships' officers at the council house walking towards the west and back again, because at the north end by the shed (*beghus*) the ordinary seamen collected. Pilots localized around the Royal Pilot Headquarters and fishermen were to be seen around their boats beached at the harbor. No one joined the group to which he did not belong. He did not care to. He would not have been allowed to.

After half an hour or an hour the groups would break up, masters, officers, and pilots heading for the "Skippers' Room" at the Old Inn or the meeting place of the Skippers' Society at "Holm's," while sailors and fishermen adjourned to the "Cellar Room" of the Old Inn or to "Schmidt's," where they were members of Unity, the society of men utilizing their premises. In these various places the men drank rum toddies and played cards until the church bells chimed six-thirty, time to go home to dinner.

The classes also emerged as corporate bodies in the social clubs. The "Old Inn" had two separate rooms where food and drink could be had, the cellar room (*Kellerstuen*) and, on the ground floor, the so-called inn room (*Krostuen*). The former was frequented by fishermen, ordinary seamen, laborers, and journeymen; the latter, by skippers, ships' officers, pilots, master craftsmen, and occasional travelers. Open from six A.M. until eleven P.M., they were frequented during the day by men seeking refreshment in the form of beer or "bitters" (*aquavitæ* or wine, with a few drops of bitters). Many of the fishermen dropped in for a morning bracer when they had finished hanging out their nets. Between four and six the rooms were filled with the men from the afternoon harbor groups, playing cards or billiards and drinking rum toddies. One did not have to pay for the privilege of playing and on Sunday afternoons twelve to fourteen card tables were often in action in the cellar room alone. In the evenings a few came to drink and play cards. Not infrequently someone with a mouth organ or accordion would play and perhaps all would join in to sing songs about Denmark or the sea—not all of them learned in school. When a man came home from a long sea voyage, especially if he were young, he might buy one or two bowls of punch into which everyone in the room could dip, spirits soon soaring in convivial reunion.

The village had, in addition, two establishments catering exclusively to a class-limited clientele. "Holm's" was a public house ordinarily used only by the maritime members of the upper class. The "Dragor Ship Owners and Shipmasters Society," more familiarly, the Skippers' Society, leased rooms in Holm's where they could meet daily for eating, drinking, games, and general socializing. Founded in the 1870's by men sharing a common level of interest in maritime shipping, by the 1890's, Skippers' Society membership had been extended to include pilots and ships' officers. Other male members of the upper class were not admitted until the first decade of the twentieth century, by which time class affiliation was no longer dependent on a marine hierarchy.

"Schmidt's" was a grocery store to which a dining room had been added on the initiative of the grocer's mother. The establishment was briefly but unsuccessfully open to all Dragorians, but became exclusive when the proprietor and some clients founded a society called the "Unity" (*Enigheden*), the purpose of which was, in effect, to provide for middle-class men facilities similar to Holm's. A man was elected to membership by popular acclama-

tion on the basis of being a "gentleman." This requirement excluded the lower class. Skippers, ships' officers, and pilots had
their own society and did not mingle socially with men who were
often their work-time subordinates. The result was a middle-class
membership made up exclusively of "ordinary people."

Winter was the season for association balls. The Skippers' Society and Unity each sponsored one for the Christmas–New Year's
holidays and a second for Shrovetide. These celebrations divided
the population socially along the neat, unyielding cleavage of its
economically based groupings. Upper-class men, women, and
children attended the Skippers' Society festivities, while middle-
class men, women, and children participated in the corresponding
activities of the Unity. The people of low class were left to organize
a scattering of informal parties for their own amusement.

With the disappearance of the merchant ships from Dragor
during the first decade of the twentieth century, the basis for reck-
oning prestige was altered. The remaining skippers, pilots, and
ship owners preserved their high status, but maritime pursuits
lost their supreme evaluation. By World War I there was no
marine employment to an extent significant for community-wide
notice of it.

With technoeconomic change, with urbanization, the old pres-
tige-class system modified, to the extinction of corporate class
groupings. The major impetus to their dissolution was that type
of occupation, the most significant criterion of organization, was
altered. Prestige instead came to attach to almost any position of
wealth and power, criteria which characterize the class-reckoning
basis of all urban Denmark.

Class stratification is ideologically unacceptable to modern
Danes, including Dragorians. As a result, it is now commonly
claimed that there are no classes in the community, or that almost
all belong to the middle class (*middelklassen*). But while the existence of classes is denied, people speak freely of "groups"
(*stænde*). Everyone is readily classified as belonging to the group
of civil servants (*embedsstand*), the worker group (*arbejdsstand*),
priest group (*præstestand*), teacher group (*lærerstand*), and so
on. As Marstrand has pointed out for Denmark as a whole, these
groups may be regarded as falling into a tripartite stratification.
Most of the population belongs to the well-defined working class;

there is a capitalist class; and a remnant is conveniently left apart as a third, undefined class.[2]

The societies with their class-limited memberships and holiday balls, the separation of Old Inn into two rooms catering to class-differentiated clienteles, and the division of the men during their afternoon promenade at the harbor—all have disappeared. At present one can speak of unified or corporate class bodies only to the limited extent that some groups (stænde), particularly the laborers and farmers, have a sense of identity of interest with groups of colleagues throughout the land, may belong to national associations, and occasionally attend national conventions and local party meetings. On the communal level, however, class is no longer the basis for the crystallization of face-to-face groups of daily significance.

Age Grades

Girls and boys in old Dragor after school played with children from their own half of town, so that two groups, "the north end" and "the south end," had a real, mutually exclusive age-ranked membership. These moieties succumbed after the turn of the century when territorial hostility shifted to that of the "ins" (Dragorians) against the "outs" (summertime dwellers from the city), and persists today as a simple sense of communal identity.

Neighborhood

The neighborhood, too, served as the basis for social groups, and Dragorians were socially intimate on the basis of being naboer and genboer. The naboer lived on either side of one's house; the genboer, across the street. Neighborhood connections by nature overlapped other institutional relationships, and were best seen at baptisms, when gifts and services reified these ties, and in the daily early-evening convocations of the women on house steps or at a convenient hot stove.

The neighborhood has undergone an ever-increasing loss of influence in social relations from the beginnings of the early influx of urban summer residents, strangers to one another and to

[2] Even Marstrand, "Den Sociale Organisation i Almindelighed," ed. Svend Dahl, Danmarks Kultur ved Aar 1940 (Copenhagen: Det Danske Forlag, 1942), pp. 132–73.

the community, to the present era of tract-home, community-apartment divisions. Neighborliness persists as a seldom fulfilled ideal in the old sections of Dragor; it is largely disdained as a potential social encumbrance in newer divisions. We found no voluntary association for diversional activities based exclusively on neighborhood. There are, however, general clubs for civic betterment, and associations whose aim is to resolve the common economic problems of houseowners or renters. In some cases these are limited to residents of a single block or housing unit.

Church

In old Dragor the church and community were coterminous in membership. The corporate nature of the community church was evidenced in holiday rituals in which the whole village, under the leadership of the priest, united to "attend the offering." In this service, social duty required the family head to carry a money contribution down the aisle of the church and to place part of it on each of two tables before the altar. One part paid the priest, the other the church musician. A family would be ashamed not to be represented in this rite.

Psychologically, the church united all villagers in the shared experience of the rites of baptism, confirmation, marriage, and internment. The Inner Mission (*Indremission*), Dragor's sole voluntary religious association, labored to reaffirm and revitalize this bond, which, in practice, lacked evangelic enthusiasm. Regular Sunday Masses were attended by only a small portion of the community, particularly by old people.

With the twentieth century, Dragor's church, like her local political institutions, underwent a progressive loss of autonomy. Legislation by the national parliament was substituted for local option, and financial responsibility shifted from the congregation as such to the communal council. The effect was catastrophic. The church was deprived of its major prop, the social obligation to seasonal attendance of all family heads. With loss of direct responsibility went a loss of individual and communal commitment. The church became just another part of the village milieu, taken for granted and forgotten.

Today, also, the psychological bond of shared religious experience has weakened with the increasing adoption of secular rites of passage.

Local Government

The domains of activity of voluntary associations themselves and of governmental bureaus and agencies have vastly increased, and their developmental adjustments in the process of urbanization show provocative parallels.

As a result of its large communal income from salvaging ships in the Sound, Dragor was authorized by the king in the eighteenth century to organize its political life in a rather unique way, enjoying independence from national control to an extent not realized by most communities. The electorate, all male property owners, elected the mayor and four councilmen who made all decisions in matters under their jurisdiction. The mayor (*foged*) was elected for life until, in 1898, his tenure was reduced to eight years. His function was primarily that of supervisor, and his vote in council was of no more weight than that of a councilman. The councilmen (*byforstandere*) were elected for four-year terms, one being elected every year. Fiscal administration was divided into four distinct treasuries—the village treasury, the harbor treasury, the school treasury, and the poor commission's treasury—and each councilman had exclusive responsibility for one of them, taking the initiative in affairs relating to it, but making no decisions independently of the full council. Mayor and councilmen were bound to fulfil their duties "on their honor as seamen and according to the old ordinances" (*paa Sømands Tro og Love og efter de gamle Vedtægter*).

The village ordinances, accepted by the electorate and authorized by the crown in 1855, gave the communal government jurisdiction in five areas. The council hired a policeman and four night watchmen, who served to warn against dangers of sudden storms and to guard against thievery in the night. The council hired a wagoner to cart off refuse from the middens. Each villager was responsible for the drainage ditch in front of his own house, and other sanitary precautions were largely individual and noncompulsory. Maintenance of the school buildings and the salaries of the schoolteachers were paid by the council. Harbor upkeep was paid for by the council and was a matter of particular interest and concern for them. Above all, they were in charge of ship salvage, a councilman being in command during the undertaking, and the council supervising the division of profits afterward according to traditional methods. The council provided some help for the poor, giving part of salvage profits to widows and keeping the poorhouse for the indigent old and infirm without close relatives.

Dragorians of that day participated in national government in that they voted for national administrators, including a man to represent them and the other inhabitants of the large area of Hvidover, which included Amager Island and part of Sealand. Only adult males possessing property had the right to vote, which was exercised by riding by horse-drawn cart to the town of Hvidover on the other side of Copenhagen. The vote was always unanimously conservative. The only nonconservative villager of the period was denied his vote by the simple expedient of not inviting him to ride on the poll-bound carriage.

National government touched the lives of Dragorians in the following ways. It required the payment of taxes, the service of each young man in the army for a period of six months, obedience to national laws, of which the only ones of importance for Dragor were the requirement of certificates for officers, skippers, and pilots. The nation provided Dragor with protection against invasion by foreign powers, postal services, law and law enforcement by the legislature and courts in Copenhagen, and other functions scarcely tangible on the local level, such as the church hierarchy and advanced education.

In 1910 the ancient form of communal government was abolished and reorganized according to the national law of 1908. The electorate has been broadened to include all adult men and women over twenty-five years of age. The new form of government provides for a mayor (now called *borgmester*) who is chairman of a council of seven councilmen (now called *byraadsmedlemer*). The major change is the extensive delegation of administrative and investigative authority to subcommittees appointed by the council to take charge of particular functions, such as education, road maintenance, and harbor control.

The responsibilities of the communal government have increased greatly and now include extensive projects in public welfare, public insurance, education, public health, public works, and so on. But with the augmented role of the communal government in local affairs has also come an increase in the influence of the national government and the concomitant decrease in the autonomy of local politicians, as more and more jurisdiction is assumed by the national ministries. In effect, the national government now requires the local government to offer a vast array of well-defined services, supervising the administration and financing of these extensive duties.

Voluntary Associations

Nineteenth-century Dragorians met some needs by formally organized voluntary associations. People united by drawing up a charter, assessing yearly dues, and electing a chairman (*formand*), secretary (*sekretær*), and treasurer (*kasserer*). Additional representatives (*representanter*) might also be elected, the whole group of officers forming a council (*bestyrelse*) whose duty it was to manage the association.

Six associations were recorded for the 1890's. The oldest was Dragor Handworkers' Sickness and Funeral Treasury (*Dragør Haandværkernes Syge- og Begravelseskasse*), founded in 1848 to provide insurance for craftsmen against loss of income due to sickness and for the expense of a funeral. The Dragor Ship Owners and Shipmasters Society of the upper class was founded in the 1870's, and the Unity of the middle class about ten years later. In the 1880's, at the instigation of a retired missionary, a local branch of the nation-wide Inner Mission (*Indremission*) was founded to revitalize religious enthusiasm. Its greatest success was in the nineties, when about three hundred and fifty men and women constructed a two-story brick "Mission House." Cork Society (*Propforeningen*) was also a local branch of a national organization. It united about thirty upper-class men of the village for the purpose of helping poor young people meet the expenses of confirmation. Its yearly dues were contributed to the cause, and the society's name derived from the practice of raising additional funds by fining members each time one was caught without a bottle cork in his pocket. Finally, Dragor's Future (*Dragørs Fremme*) was founded in 1887 by the postman, locally famed as a man of letters, to prepare the village for the breakdown of the old economy in the face of technological developments. It sought, first, a railroad to provide better contact with Copenhagen (the promotion campaign of the society, including pressure-group tactics in the capital, played a part in the laying of the railroad in 1907); second, tourist trade; and, finally, a tuberculosis sanatorium to provide local employment. No hospital was constructed, but the tourist trade successfully developed. The major economic change, however, was the inclusion of the local population in the labor market of greater Copenhagen, a development hastened by regular train service and other transportational developments.

The viability of the six associations during the new century was weak. The Unity died along with other manifestations of class solidarity. The Skippers' Society put off its demise by appealing to prestige, extending its membership to become a purely social club for people of higher income. It is now moribund. Dragor's Future grew less and less active as its leaders grew older. Its projects were relegated to other groups, and it finally disbanded in 1931. The Cork Society became extinct during the first World War. Dragor's Handworkers Sickness and Funeral Treasury is still operative but offers only supplementary benefits, since security against illness and unemployment is now a function of the national government, under whose administration most private insurance societies in Denmark have been absorbed.

The old associations did not fare well as time progressed, but new ones appeared. Especially in the solution of problems related to economic adjustment, expansion, and leisure, the voluntary association became a social medium more and more resorted to. After World War II, especially, new societies proliferated, utilizing an essentially unchanged pattern of formal internal organization.

In 1904 the fishermen formed a society (*Dragør Fiskeriforening*) to cooperate in transporting fish to the market, replacing the old system of individual arrangements, in dealing with the village council and persuading it to reserve a special section of the harbor for the exclusive use of Dragorian fishermen and to restrict for their use beach areas where boiling vats and net racks were kept.

Ship salvage had traditionally provided an income to Dragorian mariners, especially during winter. Whereas formerly the men participated simply by virtue of village residence, by 1921 they organized the Salvage Guild (*Bjaergelav*) to allot work equitably among local mariners and to exclude outsiders from the coveted windfalls.

Local brotherhoods of trade unions and professional organizations were formed. Where membership was small, craftsmen and artisans were absorbed into existing Copenhagen groups. Even goose keepers formed an association. As far back as her history goes, Dragorians had kept geese, and Dragor is known nationally for the flocks that usurp streets, beaches, and yards as a public aviary. By 1940 criticism of the noise and dirt of the free-roaming birds reached such dimensions that the village council was prepared summarily to prohibit the keeping of fowl. The goose keepers responded by forming the Dragor Fowl Society (*Dragør Fjaerkraeforening*), whose representatives effected a compromise with the village council. Geese continue to have the freedom of the village, but the society has responsibility for sanitation and their proper housing.

With urbanization, Dragorians found new diversions and more time for them. Young people especially have come to have leisure in the late afternoons and evenings now that a dawn-to-dusk work day is no longer the custom. At the same time, many traditional activities disappeared. The Wednesday and Saturday promenades, which formerly attracted the entire community, ended, and the leisure activities of the domestic family no longer center around the single oil lamp. For Dragor's youth the street corner or the hot-dog stand has become the focal point after dark. The earliest organized attempt to rechannel activities was the sponsorship by interested citizens of Boy Scouts, Girl Scouts, Sunday-school classes, and the Dragor Sport Club, with its playing fields, tennis courts, and clubhouse. In 1956 Dragor's communal council granted money and personnel for a youth center to bring boys and girls in off the streets to participate in varied activities.

In 1937 a number of women formed the Dragor Mothers' Society (*Dragør Husmødrenesforening*), with the purpose of sponsoring lectures and instruction in the art of homemaking. In three years its membership reached a peak of two hundred and fifty, extending beyond the business-professional class, its nucleus, to include a number of working-class wives. After World War II it re-formed, the same ladies, now middle-aged with grown children, continuing as a small club of matrons meeting infrequently to have coffee and hear lectures on social problems. Today's young mother is most likely to seek instruction in one of the many courses given in the local adult night school.

Organized diversion for the adults of Dragor is less ambitious than for her youth but quite widespread. As family men abandoned their toddies and card games in the class-separated rooms of the inn, they sought intimacy in small groups, and these often crystallized into permanent but informal leisure unions, their members meeting regularly at one another's homes in round-robin fashion. The women, too, have their groups, but they appear not to be more numerous than the men's. A few are of mixed membership. Organized adult activities, sponsored by the communal government, center on the school and include a winter movie series as well as music evenings. Educational and recreational courses in the evening school are also government sponsored. There is notably no parent-teacher association. Every summer the old people, who have never formed associations, are given a day's outing by the communal council.

In the apartment houses built on the south side of the village after 1945, units were individually owned, and the building was managed by a hired manager under corporate-trust arrangement. Residents, nevertheless, found it expedient to form associations, to elect officers, and to meet regularly to discuss and vote upon such problems as the allotment of time and space in the communal washing facilities and the control of noise. Similarly, homeowners in the "villa" section north of the old village, formed an association to determine and defend their interests. Finally, associations, usually small and ephemeral, were founded for a variety of specific-interest purposes. A mason, a businessman, and the village doctor formed the still-active Dragor Museum Society (*Dragør Museums-forening*) to acquire and preserve local cultural heirlooms. In the year of our field study (1956–57), a group of four was formed at the behest of a deceased man of wealth to advise on the construction of the new church entrance financed by the legacy. In this year another group disbanded after achieving its purpose in preventing the addition of an unesthetic fourth story to a new building in the heart of town.

In Sum

The voluntary association is extremely pliant. Easily founded, it is free to adjust with amoeba-like fluidity to a flood of problems beyond the scope or ken of other institutions or any combination of them. Its job done, it can go out of business without consequences beyond projects at hand. Danish voluntary associations and forms of government share an organizational structure specifically contrived to facilitate and precipitate change by providing effective, policy-making leaders responsive to their electorate. In contrast, the Dragorian household after a half century of economic change cannot revert to the familial work unit and, like the church, does not know on what basis it can now reallocate its declining authority. The rigid class system of the nineties, the tight little neighborhood, even the exacting northside-southside age groups—all declined in the face of change, apparently because their perpetuation was dependent upon the maintenance of equilibrium in an established social ordering.

In this process of change, associations and governmental agencies grew primarily by assuming tasks formerly either nonexistent or so vastly simpler as to have been qualitatively different. Thus, the government has taken over the now elaborate system of sewage disposal, production and distribution of gas, water, and electricity, and traffic control, while associations have been important in dealing with juvenile delinquency, the use of new leisure time, industrialization of the village, cooperative enterprises in fishing, and so on.

To a lesser extent, their increased prominence was due to the shifting of functions from other institutions. Thus, care of the aged was largely a family concern in the nineties with communal responsibility limited toward those without kinship ties. Indigents survived upon gleaning and traditionally preferred handouts within the neighborhood, with only sporadic reliance upon the community's Poor Commission's Treasury. Village sanitation was largely the responsibility of each household head and maintained by families, with local government obligations limited primarily to the carting off of several refuse middens. Care in sickness beyond that possible within the domestic family used to be largely left to one's neighbors or relatives.

The voluntary association meets the exigencies of change by uniting people for action on the basis of any shared interest, whether the resultant union coincides with other groupings or cuts a swathe through them. The ultimate result is not just a predominance of special interest associations but a pronounced tendency for other institutions, especially of class, neighborhood, and age, to lose all corporate unity other than that expressed in associations, so that they become, in effect, no more than part of the large number of special-interest groups. Indeed, when the rationale of these older institutions decreases, the remaining basis for their social coherence is as the points of crystallization of voluntary associations.

The ties of kinship and propinquity do not, in the city, necessarily or even commonly unite people with a shared goal. Institutions based upon these ties are thereby less usable in mobilizing social action. Governmental units, although local, provide an exception in their demonstrated ability to take effective action for special purposes. A community or nation does this by virtue of including the group as part of its total population. Thus it does not constitute a special interest group; it encompasses it. Voluntary associations may thus be expected to be more directly responsive to certain special needs. We found that they assumed functions normally beyond the concern of governmental agencies (i.e., the satisfaction of diverse avocational interests—jazz club, kayak club), or not as yet of sufficient importance to warrant active governmental intervention (i.e., Dragor's association to limit the height of new construction), or, finally, inadequately controlled by the government or by other institutions, including the family—such as control and prevention of juvenile delinquency.

The impetus to multiplication and elaboration of associations was as much socially linked with the patterns of the community's past as with the more recent urbanism. Because they had existed for at least a couple of generations, were established with pride, and successfully maintained and directed social participation without disrupting the existent social structure, associations were seized upon as a traditional social device to cope with the extra-institutional problems that arose with the village's twentieth-century economic and cultural revolution. Even more conclusively, modern communal government developed out of a tradition of local self government.

10: Sexual Behavior in Perspective

THE extent to which Scandinavia may be regarded as a single culture area with respect to sexual habits is yet to be determined.[1] There are several selective studies, few regional ones. In Norway, Melbye had a questionnaire on sexual problems filled out by four hundred students who had been interned by the Germans in February, 1945.[2] In Sweden, Hofsten made a study of sex life based upon a questionnaire of one thousand recruits (half in their twenties and half in their forties) as well as the sexual behavior of 314 women as determined in interviews with their physicians, seven doctors participating.[3] Danish studies include that of 250 married couples recruited through a newspaper advertisement asking for volunteers willing to answer personal questions of marital and family circumstances.[4] Rather specialized studies were also carried out by Hartmann, who interviewed 227 women who had been checked for venereal disease during World War II after having sexual intercourse with German soldiers, and by Hoffmeyer, who interrogated 426 women seeking maternity aid in Copenhagen.[5] The most comprehensive work is that of Kirsten

[1] This chapter has appeared as "Sexual Behaviour and Urbanization in a Danish Village," *Southwestern Journal of Anthropology*, XVI (1960), 93–109.

[2] C. Melbye, "Studentmoral," *Universitas*, No. 7–8, (Oslo: 1946).

[3] I. von Hofsten, "Ungdomens sexualvanor," *Svenska Läkartidenda*, XLI (1944), 1158.

[4] H. Gottschalk, *Moderne Ægteskabsproblemer* (Copenhagen: 1947).

[5] G. Hartmann, *The Girls They Left Behind* (Copenhagen: 1946); H. Hoffmeyer, "Anticonception," *Ugeskrift for Læger*, CXIII (1951), 569 ff.

Auken, who intensively interviewed 315 Danish women on all aspects of their sexual background.[6]

In discussing the selection of informants for her study, Auken made the following observation:

In comparison with the population of large countries such as the U.S.A., a country like Denmark has a quite uniform demographic composition. It is a question of a restricted geographical whole; broadly regarded, the population belongs to a single race. Everyone belongs, practically speaking, to the same church communion. Schooling is very uniform, at least as concerns grammar school. There are smaller economic differences than in most other nations. Even the transition from country to city is smooth, since rural inhabitants in recent decades have become more and more urbanized. However one would judge these circumstances, it is indeed clear that by international comparison it is a question of a very homogeneous population.[7]

Auken's observations concur with more specific comparisons, as shown below. Dragor is thus not singled out as distinctive in its sexual mores and practices, but is simply the specific reference here for generalized Danish and Scandinavian practices.

The Meeting of the Sexes

In the day-to-day life of the village, the restrictions of work tended to separate the sexes. Yet often, despite job demands, nubile girls and young men found the occasion to cross paths, loitering here and there around the village while others, less romantically impelled, were busy with familiar chores. They also met, however, at times and places and under circumstances more formally defined by tradition.

Of these traditions, the "promenade" recurred most frequently. Wednesday and Saturday evenings, weather permitting (which would exclude the winter season), found most villagers indulging in a ritual-like exercise on the main street of the village (*Kongevejen*). For an hour or more in the sun-bright evening, young people and old walked back and forth between the harbor and the church. Girls walked arm in arm. Boys, participating with less restraint, formed groups of their own, following the girls sometimes, and taking the initiative in conversation, lancing comments and witticisms at girls who caught their interest. These were girls whom

[6] Kirsten Auken, *Undersøgelser over Unge Kvinders Sexuelle Adfærd* (Copenhagen: Rosenkilde og Bagger, 1953).

[7] Ibid., p. 48. Authors' translation.

the boys had known from infancy, often close age mates, but they were rediscovering them now as "girl friends" (*veninder*). The girls reacted sometimes shyly, sometimes sharply to this virile new interest not yet fully distinguished from the play interest of childhood. Their awkward, yet pointed, exchanges were in contrast with the obvious mutual attachment of promenading engaged pairs and the subdued deportment of the married couples.

The celebrations of the yearly cycle of holidays and the rites of passage also provided opportunities for the meeting of the sexes. The Christmas, New Year, and Shrovetide balls, which congregated the inhabitants according to class affiliations, offered the chance for couples to pair off and were the occasion for the beginning of many liaisons.

Finally, a public dance was held every Sunday night in one of the local inns or in a neighboring village. At a cost of thirty-five øre for the girl, seventy øre for the boy, one could dance from eight P.M. until midnight to the music of a small horn band. Although the girls had no refreshments, the boys drank beer and rum toddies. The early part of the evening was devoted to round dancing in a rather decorous manner. Between dances the girls sat on a bench along one side of the room, the boys along the other side. When the music started, the boys crossed the room to the girls of their choice, bowed and escorted the girls to the dance floor, usually in complete silence. After the dance, the boy followed the girl to her bench, said "thank you," bowed and returned to the company of the other young men. As the evening wore on, however, round dancing was abandoned for the isolation of couples embraced in the dancing of polkas and mazurkas, and the more daring young girls shared a drink with the men. Couples trying to stay together between dances, however, were frustrated by the intimacy of the group.

Young people did not usually have their parents' permission to attend these public dances until they were several years past confirmation, generally around eighteen years of age. Some of the boys became inebriated, and it was partly for this reason that many parents were reluctant to have their children attend. Some parents also feared undue intimacy between the sexes in clandestine rendezvous after the dance, and so forbade their daughters to go. Most boys, however, generally managed to get their parents' consent or attended without permission. As a rule, the girls from skipper or pilot families, the upper class, were never permitted to participate in these public dances, and the informal boycott of them was a matter of pride and propriety to their families.

It was almost exclusively through these dances that the community's youth came into formal social contact with neighboring villagers of their own age, and the evenings often ended in free-for-all fights between boys from the different villages. Other contacts were less boisterous, and intermarriages occurred, more often with young people from fishing families in coastal villages than with those from the inland farms, who by virtue of their Dutch ancestry and near endogamy considered our villagers inferior socially as well as economically. While intermarriage was also frequent with fishing families from more distant harbors on the Sound in Sweden and Norway as well as in Denmark, these unions resulted from the contacts of young men in irregular temporary residence in the various fishing centers during fishing seasons.

Many social activities were suspected in 1914 and after the war some customs were not revived. Among the war victims were the promenade and the seasonal village balls, activities which joined villagers of all ages. Young people turned instead to street-corner socializing, school activities, and commercial entertainment.

The most prominent survival is the week-end dance, now as then a business undertaking appealing exclusively to the youth group. Dancing behavior, however, has changed. After the first decade of the new century, folk dancing was replaced by paired-couple dancing, and the dances attract a heterogeneous crowd in which the group cohesion of the old days is much weakened. As of old, however, the dances are notorious as centers where liaisons are reputedly made leading to casual sexual intimacy. As a result, many girls, regardless of class lines, are forbidden to attend. Boys too are frequently denied parental permission because of the heavy beer drinking and prevalent drunkenness. The opinion that these dances are undesirable for young people is now much more widespread, but there are still no definite sanctions against those attending and parents' wishes are often ignored.

In the evolution between the wars of separate activities for the young and a freer status of the young man and woman, a new element has emerged to partly replace the group diversions of the nineties—dating. Pairing off for an evening at the movies, a public dance, or a walk—activities once the privilege only of engaged couples—is now the pattern for new acquaintances. Places of amusement in Copenhagen, now regularly attended by dating couples, are also popular centers for the rapprochement of young men and women who are strangers, not only to one another, but to families and friends as well.

In spite of an increased independence within the group of individuals and couples, the peer group functions for youth as a primary reference unit. And as a reference group, youth is now left isolated from other age grades by the disappearance of older joint activities.

Courtship and Marriage

Various types of courting relationships were traditional to the village. The first clearly defined stage of pairing off was marked by the couple more or less exclusively seeking out each other's company. Such a couple were regarded as "going-together" (*gaa med*). Recognition was primarily by their age mates and only indirectly by adults. Parents only acquiesced by not openly opposing the activity. "Going-together" could end in dissolution or advance to the next type, that of engagement or betrothal (*forlovet*).

Betrothal was a serious thing, and as a rule occurred only once in a person's lifetime. In spite of the seriousness attaching to it, the *forlovet* relationship was established quietly and without ceremony, after a period of going together for perhaps several months, but more commonly several years. The girl was generally at least sixteen years of age, the boy twenty. Only their families were specifically advised of their plans to marry, and a marriage date was rarely set.

Engagement ordinarily lasted at least one year and rarely more than five, at which time the couple established a new type of relationship, that of being "ring engaged" (*ringforlovet*) which itself could continue from a few months to a few years. Ring engagement was initiated when concrete plans could be made to cope with the economic demands of marriage. The couple bought two simple gold bands, each with the fiancés' initials inscribed on the inside, and showed the rings to their parents— first to the parents of the girl. The rings were worn on the right index finger, and continued to be worn in the same way after marriage. Although the ring engagement might be a surprise announcement, there was usually at least a hint of it in the air and often it was carefully planned and widely anticipated. A simple little coffee party with rum toddies for the men was commonly held in the home of the girl's parents.

The ring engagement intensified and solidified the relationship between the young couple and anticipated relatives by marriage. The fiancé, who may or may not have previously eaten dinner at the home of his betrothed, now became a regular guest at the table of his future parents-in-law. The girl, too, dined regularly at the home of her fiancé's family. Although the practice may have begun during the period of engagement, it was now an unqualified rule that the parents of the betrothed should be called by the kinship terms proper to a married couple—"father-in-law" (*svigerfar*) and "mother-in-law" (*svigermor*)—in address as well as reference, with no modification to indicate that the marriage had not yet taken place. Similarly, the terms "brother-in-law" (*svoger*) and "sister-in-law" (*svigerinde*) were used in referring to the siblings of the betrothed, although in address first names were used. The betrothed were now so much a part of one another's family that each was always invited to the other's family occasions, such as baptisms, weddings, confirmations, birthdays, anniversaries, funerals, as well as to Christmas festivities and other seasonal parties.

It was desirable, and common, for the couple to acquire the necessary equipment before setting up housekeeping. The girl may have been accumulating things for years, embroidering tablecloths, knitting towels, and so on. But now the couple entered upon the more difficult task of getting furniture. Ideally they were to acquire before marriage enough to furnish a whole house or apartment, and minimally, a bedroom and front room. Generally, the furniture for one room was acquired before starting on the next, first the bedroom, then the front room.

The final relationship entered into was marriage.

The types of institutionalized relationships enumerated for the nineties still exist, but there have been significant changes. The general trend to greater individual freedom in social attachments is associated with a greater number of alliances per individual. There are many more brief encounters and less permanence, though a higher frequency, of "going-together" relationships. Engagement is now less stable, so that individuals are commonly betrothed several times before the final ring engagement and marriage, and the ring betrothal, formerly binding, may now be broken. The economic aspects of ring engagement are less pressing. Couples can now obtain furniture with only a down payment and a committal to make monthly installments. Ring engagement continues, however, to inaugurate intimate social relations with future affinal kin.

Although the church wedding ritual remains essentially unchanged, other customs formerly associated with weddings have been greatly simplified to conform to standards set in the capital. Many now forego the church rite for a civil ceremony. After approximately 1910 it ceased to be the custom to "go around and invite"; the wedding party became limited to a single day; relatives stopped acting as "cooks"; and the parade through the village ended.

Intimacy

The majority of the villagers of the nineties experienced premarital intercourse; the girls generally only with one person, the man they ultimately married. It was assumed that a ring-engaged couple would have sexual relations, although no regular, sanctioned opportunity was provided them and they did not openly live together. This intimacy was regarded, even by the parents of the couple, as normal and expectable and it was assumed that they would find occasion for it. Opportunities varied. The boy might quietly enter the girl's room if she slept apart from brothers and sisters; they might go late at night to the park or harbor by the beached boats.

In 1880 Rubin and Westergaard found that in fifty country parishes two thirds of the brides had a child before, or within a month after, the wedding. This custom derived from a still earlier period when cohabitation was sanctioned by betrothal rather than marriage. It was usual among the sixteenth-century Danish peasants for a man to live with his fiancée (fæstemø) on their future farm up to six months before the wedding. The wedding was itself only a voluntary, optional repetition of the vows of betrothal until 1582, when it became mandatory, and the engagement was not stricken from the law books as the official inauguration of married life until 1799.[8] A hundred years later the sentiment was still widespread that sexual life began with engagement.

In other parts of Scandinavia the engagement was similarly regarded as sanctioning sexual relations. Ødegaard maintains that it is an ancient Norwegian custom for villagers to inaugurate sex life while engaged, with the wedding possibly precipitated by the onset of pregnancy, while Wikman and Berg and Svensson describe similar traditions in nineteenth-century Sweden.[9]

In the contemporary village, coitus in ring betrothal is unofficially condoned as of old, but it has become more clearly acceptable for informal betrothal as well. Since sexual intimacy is sanctioned for betrothed couples, and since betrothal is simply an oral agreement between the two young people costing neither time nor money, it has become common for a person to be "engaged" several times before marriage in order to clothe the act with respectability. In recent years "to be engaged" so nearly implies "to engage in sexual intercourse," that the term has become blurred; often when referring to betrothal one is referring rather to a couple being sexually intimate.

During the 1940's Auken intensively interviewed a random sample of 315 Danish women about their sex lives. Her findings indicate that our village continues to be representative of general Danish practice. Of the 315 women twenty years of age or older, 31 (9.8 per cent) have never had sexual intercourse. Of the remaining 284, 98.6 per cent indicated that the first coitus was outside of marriage. The surviving role of engagement as inaugurating married life is suggested, however, by the finding that 51.7 per cent of the women were either engaged or ring engaged at the time of their first copulation, and 65.1 per cent believed that their first affair would lead to marriage. Fifty per cent (143 women) had had two or more affairs of sexual intimacy, and of this group 26.7 per cent were engaged to the second man with whom they had sexual relations. Of the 21.8 per cent of experi-

[8] Ibid., p. 154.
[9] Ø. Ødegaard, *Samlivets naturlære* (Oslo: 1941); K. Rob, V. Wikman, *Die Einleitung der Ehe, eine vergleichend ethno-soziologische Untersuchung über die Vorstufe der Ehe in den Sitten des Schwedishchen Volkstums* (Åbo: Das Institut für Nordische Ethnologie an der Åbo Akademie, 1937); G. Berg and S. Svensson, *Svensk Bondekultur* (Stockholm: 1934).

enced women who had had three or more affairs, only 8.1 per cent were engaged.[10]

The Youth Commission report of 1952 for the whole of Denmark is equally pertinent.

> There is no doubt that the official sex morality is only lived up to by a very restricted portion of the young people, and that the vast majority of young boys as well as young girls inaugurate sexual relations before marriage. Many, however, do it with serious scruples and consideration. A significant number, moreover, only have sexual intercourse before marriage with the person whom they later marry.[11]

Sex and Family

The basic socioeconomic unit of the 1890's was the nuclear family. Divorce was difficult to obtain legally and strongly censured by local opinion. The divorced person was a rarity, was not received in many homes, and was excluded from membership in some social groups. Adultery in the village was regarded as highly reprehensible. It was so covert and rare that incidence of it is undocumented for the last decade of the century. (The patronage of prostitutes in foreign ports had no direct relevance for village life.)

The integrity of the family was further guarded by the severe ostracism of unmarried mothers. A woman encountered no difficulty, however, if a pregnancy occurred before marriage but in betrothal, especially ring betrothal, and couples hitherto only spuriously joined were pressed to announce engagement when a pregnancy occurred. This stratagem and sanctions levied against illegitimate childbirth served, though only by implicit extension, to delimit premarital promiscuity to the established channels.

The current premarital sex code is correlated with a profound alteration in the character of the marital union. Divorce is common and adultery is no longer rare nor so covert as in the nineties. Ten per cent of the married women in Auken's national sample admitted to adultery.[12] The sanctions on unwed mothers have greatly diminished, and illegitimate children are no longer a rarity.

The nuclear family is still the basic social unit of the com-

[10] Auken, pp. 159, 170.

[11] "Ungdomen og Fritiden" (Copenhagen: Betænkning afgivet at Ungdomskommissionen, 1952). Authors' translation.

[12] Auken, p. 214.

munity even though it is no longer a primary work unit. The daily dispersal of its members and other urban-derived exigencies have watered down its integrity, however, and the family shows significantly mounting impotency in the supervision and care of its members. As in the rest of Denmark, broken homes are associated with personal and social maladjustments.

These problems are being met with characteristic Scandinavian practicality. New sanctions have been invoked in the form of national laws regulating divorce, limiting abortions, and punishing adultery. They are notable for their limited effectiveness. The problem is also being met by structural-functional adjustments. Institutional care is provided for unwed mothers and unwanted children, and broken homes receive governmental supervision and aid. These adjustments bring only ameliorative relief, however, and the malfunctioning modern family remains a serious sociocultural problem.

Sex and Class

Since marriage might derive from an unplanned conception, the upper economic stratum had a greater interest in inhibiting sexual license than the lower. It was economically preferable for the former to restrict marital unions to comparable occupational categories by careful marital management. This was accomplished by a more careful surveillance of upper-class girls. They were forbidden to attend the Sunday-night public dances, for it was generally believed that young people regularly paired off to spend an intimate hour in the town park, on the beach, or elsewhere. The female component of the public-dance set was middle and lower class. This is not to say that parents of these classes were without concern about the sexual activities of their daughters. On the contrary, in moral matters they typically related to upper-class behavior as an ideal. Even in the lowest class, many would not allow a girl to attend until she was seventeen or eighteen, and even then meted out harsh discipline if the girl came home later than a quarter past twelve, fifteen minutes after the last dance. The feature which distinguished class attitude was that upper-class parents were unwilling to risk the involvement of their daughters in even the chance of an ill-advised sexual experience, whereas the lower classes more willingly compromised with the desire for amusement.

Parents of all classes now have less authority over their childrens' activities than formerly, yet one still finds upper-class homes in which considerable restrictions are maintained.

In modern Scandinavia as a whole, evidence points to a tendency for sexual behavior to be more inhibited in the upper classes than in the lower. Thus, Jonsson divided his Swedish sample into three classes, and found that sexual intercourse before the age of twenty was experienced by 45.5 per cent of the upper-class, 69.5 per cent of the middle-class, and 80.1 per cent of the lowest-class men.[13] In Denmark, Auken similarly found that sexual relations begin earlier in the lower classes than in the upper. She also noted the tendency for a larger percentage of women with more than one affair to occur in the lower than in the upper classes. For example, of sexually experienced women, 64.0 per cent to 73.3 per cent of women whose fathers were academic people, independent business men, or permanent civil servants had had only one affair, whereas those from the working class with only one affair amounted to only 36.2 per cent.[14]

Even if sexual inhibition continues to characterize the upper class of our community, however, a lessened effect must be noted in the sense that the upper class now constitutes a smaller proportion of the total population, since both upper and lower classes have shrunk in size relative to the growing middle class. The upper class, it also seems clear, has lost ground to the middle as the exponent of ideal behavior.

Sex and Religion

Christian belief was accepted without question, and without enthusiasm. Only a small portion of the community attended regular Sunday mass. The church, however, was periodically prominent. Virtually every one was baptized, confirmed, married, and buried by the priest. Most of the villagers attended the Christmas, New Year, and Easter services when public offerings were made by the head of each family.

Religion was cherished for its ritual and for its solace and comfort. The characterization of God as an avenger, a discipli-

[13] G. Jonsson, "Sexualvanor hos svensk ungdom," *Ungdomen möter samhället* (Stockholm: Ungdomsvårdskommittens slutbetänkande, 1951), pp. 205–13.
[14] Auken, p. 64.

narian, or a judge appears to have had small acceptance for the average villager. His language sometimes violated the second commandment (as defined by Martin Luther's Little Catechism); his Sunday activities the third; his thoughts, speech, and actions might betray the ninth and tenth; and his premarital sexual activities the sixth—but these transgressions were equally regarded with almost ingenuous equanimity. With respect to sexual behavior in particular it was commonly felt that the young people were too weak to resist such strong natural impulses, and that so long as no harm was done to anyone it should not be regarded as a matter of serious concern. Religion played an important role in social life and was a conventional refuge in moments of need. But its communal role did not necessarily impose ethical proscriptions or moral sanctions on behavior.

In the present community, church activity has declined further. Confirmation, marriage, and interment are now frequently purely civil ceremonies, and even seasonal church attendance has fallen off. The minor role of the church in the community, as in all of Denmark and Scandinavia, is associated with a lack of widespread religious influence upon interpersonal relationships. The minority of active Christians, however, do place moral restrictions upon sexual behavior, although they do not necessarily regard sexual intimacy in engagement as sinful.

The inhibiting effect of religion on the *active* Christian has been stressed in a Danish and a Norwegian study. Auken observed that of the 250 members of her Danish sample who gave usable answers, premarital sexual intercourse was considered justifiable by 92.2 per cent of the nonreligious women, 83.1 per cent of the passively religious, and only 62.7 per cent of the actively religious. Similarly, the opinion that sexual intercourse was justifiable without being engaged to be married was held by 51.6 per cent of the nonreligious, 30.8 per cent of the passively religious, and 20.5 per cent of the actively religious.[15] Melbye found in Norway that of the 400 students studied, premarital intercourse had been experienced by one third of the inactive Christians but only by one tenth of those with a positive religious orientation.[16] These findings for Denmark as a whole and for Norway are in basic agreement with observations made in Dragor, but should not

[15] Auken, pp. 369–73.
[16] Melbye.

obscure the fact that the number of active or positive Christians is not large, and hence the moral influence of the church is not great.

Sanctions Against Promiscuity

Sexual activity was regarded as natural and therefore not innately wicked. Only the blatantly promiscuous girl who indulged simultaneously or serially in a number of affairs was ostracized, she and her relatives subjected to gossip and shame. Marriage, however, terminated moral reproach, which in any case, was never extended to the children. Only in cases of persistent defiance of social customs would a woman be subjected to long-term ostracism. One woman who had two illegitimate children was avoided by her neighbors and publicly chastised by the priest when her second baby was baptized. It seems clear on the whole that the primary social irritant was children without families rather than sexual experimentation. Adultery was regarded as unthinkable.

Although religious or social ethics were largely ineffectual, ignorance and fear did inhibit promiscuity. Girls were kept from knowledge of anything having to do with sex. Mothers were careful never to undress completely in front of their children, and even the most elementary facts of conception, pregnancy, and birth were often unknown to premarriage girls. One mother of six reported that at the time she was carrying her first child, conceived during her engagement, she did not even know "where it would come out."

On the other hand, it was common knowledge that women and infants died in childbirth. No method of pain relief was used by the village midwife, who was notorious for her indifference toward hygiene and solace. Her dolorous counsel to the woman in labor was "it will get worse." Large families of eight, ten, or twelve children were nevertheless customary despite anxiety and awareness of the economic hardship entailed in their upbringing. Yet, contraceptive measures were rarely employed, and fear of the physical and economic consequences of pregnancy appears of itself significantly to have discouraged intimacy only in informal unions. Her socially instilled duty to submissive obedience appears to have been the major consideration in a woman's consent to first coitus, a duty felt in betrothal as well as marriage.

Her own biological inclinations, then as now, would not normally seem to have been decisively motivating in the inauguration of sexual intercourse.[17]

Reliable estimates of the effect of these sanctions were impossible to obtain. Some informants describe a youth of considerable sexual experience while others insist upon the former chastity of themselves and the majority of their acquaintances. Upper-class informants frequently attribute a sexual laxity to the lower class, which some of the latter deny.

Casual encounters without even pretense of sufficient longevity to be called betrothal, while probably not typical of the majority of young people, are now nonetheless frequent, and sexual intimacy in a succession of engagements is common. These increases in overt premarital sexuality are correlated with an extensive breakdown of the sanctions formerly imposed and by a new predominance of the sanction of the youth group on a promiscuous moral code.

The effectiveness of the sanctions of fear and ignorance was largely destroyed by a new knowledge. Respect for knowledge is a generic Danish trait which facilitated the spread of new ideas, in part on the communal level through schools and public programs. Medical developments dissipated fear of childbirth, and developments in contraception diminished the possibility of unwanted pregnancy. Knowledge of contraceptives is fully disseminated. Girls as young as fourteen or fifteen seek professional help in their use. Male as well as female devices are explained and distributed by state outlets which advertise in color in the local cinema. Should pregnancy occur, governmental institutions provide for the unmarried mother during gestation and parturition and can arrange for the child to be given in subsequent adoption. Most girls, however, appear to prefer an abortion which, although difficult to get legally, is often otherwise manageable for a fee. (Fenger and Lindhardt note an enormous increase in the number of abortions in Denmark as a whole.) [18] In this new atmosphere of unrestricted knowledge, the community smiles indulgently at the naïveté and secrecy of its nineteenth-century years.

The separation of youth activities from other age groups facili-

---

[17] Auken, p. 180; Hoffmeyer, p. 569.
[18] M. Fenger and M. Lindhardt, "On antallet af aborter i Danmark 1940–1950," *Ugeskrift for Læger* 114 (1952), 617.

tates enforcement within their social circle of the ethic of sexual liberality. In their social isolation, the sanction of ostracism that formerly operated on the communal level to enforce traditional conformity now operates within the youth group for conformity to the ideals as expressed, in part, in movies and magazines. Hoffmeyer made the following remarks about his Danish sample of girls seeking help in Copenhagen:

> A majority of the women who seek maternity help (*mødrehjælpen*) had their first sexual experience at the age of 17 or 18. Not a few women appear to have submitted to it unwillingly—although for a number the unwillingness was camouflaged by a drive to be up to date and to satisfy themselves, which is "good tone" in the circle of friends. One has the impression that a spontaneous need for early sexual intercourse rarely exists. On the contrary, many seem to have been characterized by ambivalent and negative attitudes towards sex.[19]

In Sum

The general evolution of sexual practices in Dragor may be regarded as typical for Denmark and representative of Scandinavia as a whole.

The types of formalized relationship continue as of old to be "going together," engagement, ring engagement, and marriage. Formerly, all but the first were serious unions, rarely broken once contracted. Ancient tradition sanctified the beginning of marital relationships during ring engagement, which was in fact the older form of marriage and constituted a permanent monogamous union. Now sexual intercourse is also widely regarded as acceptable in simple engagement. Both forms of engagement, however, have become unstable. Modern individuals are commonly engaged several times and ring engagement may be broken without notable social consequences. The result is a tacit approval of serial sexual liaisons and a *de facto* system of trial marriage.

The development of the new patterns of sexual behavior necessitated the breakdown of former sanctions against sexual license. Premarital promiscuity was formerly discouraged in the village's ostracism of loose girls and unwed mothers, and by the inhibiting effect of fear and ignorance of sex and childbirth. Ostracism was also effective against divorce and adultery. Now, education has mollified fear and effaced ignorance. Public opinion is less con-

[19] Hoffmeyer, p. 571. Authors' translation.

cerned with sexual transgressions and unable in any case to ostracize effectively the urban individual who is no longer socially limited to the local face-to-face community. Loss of former sanctions was correlated with the social isolation of the youth group, which finds diversion in activities that contrast with the nineteenth-century in completely excluding adults and small children. This modern youth society enforces its own ethic of sexual freedom by imposing ostracism within the age grade.

How is this new morality, this *de facto* system of trial marriage, working out? An unbiased judgment, of course, is difficult. But whatever one's over-all conclusion, at least one area of related social disorganization is notable. The nuclear family, the basic socioeconomic unit of the village, was formerly protected by strong sanctions against divorce, adultery, and unwed motherhood. These practices, however, are now condoned and common, and constitute both symptoms and sources of family instability. This lost family integrity, deriving in part at least from changed sexual practices, constitutes a serious dysfunction insofar as the family continues to occupy a key position in the social structure.

11: Change and Conflict

IN the 1890's Dragor, Denmark, was, as it had been for two centuries, a harbor community, its existence so bound up with the sea that the union of its culture and its maritime-fishing economy seemed inextricable. Despite its geographic proximity to the capital and a history of centuries of exposure to potential innovations from sea traffic, Dragor's inhabitants were isolated and conservative. The life of the city dweller was remote from them.

Yet change came, swiftly in consideration of the cultural tenacity of the past, and so pervasively that few aspects of the village's cultural inventory emerged without profound alteration. And what is yet more striking, the adjustment from maritime village to urban annex has been accomplished in a few decades and has been embraced by an entire population *virtually without sociocultural conflict*. How was it achieved?

The early heralds of change were not auspicious. Technological progress affected every local industry. The final decay of the once great sailing fleet took place shortly after the turn of the century. Sound fishermen had increasing difficulty competing for local and world markets as developments in transportation made distant, richer fishing grounds profitable. The ancient home occupations of weaving and open-air linen bleaching could not compete with new factories. Shipwrecks, long a source of salvage bounty, became less frequent and required expensive specialized equipment.

Yet little by little the technological progress that brought economic crisis to the village also brought its solution. In the course of two decades Dragor found itself a suburb of Copenhagen with its economic base in the capital city.

Immigrants from Copenhagen accounted for the growth of the community. At the turn of the century the first Copenhageners came as summer residents. They built small villas in the northern end of town which they left uninhabited during the greater part of the year. In 1907 a railroad was built between the capital and Dragor, significantly augmenting the suburban exodus. Although railroad travel was not cheap, it was reasonable enough for people in the professional classes and it was fast. Thus it became feasible for the villa people to remodel their houses and live all year round in this beautiful little harbor town. The real expansion, however, waited until after World War II. By that time the need for housing was acute in the capital and it was practical to meet this need by the construction of suburban communities, particularly in view of the developments that had taken place in the areas of communication and transportation.

The train, buses, bicycles, and private motorized vehicles which permitted the arrival of Copenhageners also permitted Dragorians to commute, an opportunity that was quickly grasped as the old forms of local occupation became unprofitable and forced the villagers to look to the city for a means of earning a living. The local people became part of this great urban labor force. Many commuted daily to the capital and others found new types of employment within Dragor's limits as a result of the increased needs of the growing community for goods and services.

Through seven hundred years of recorded history Dragor had habitually increased its population by the immigration of outsiders. Throughout the Hansa period until approximately 1500 the population had been almost completely transient—summer residents coming from all over Denmark, from Germany, Holland, Sweden, and elsewhere. Subsequent centuries witnessed Dragor's growth as a permanent settlement, including individuals from Sweden, Norway, other parts of Denmark and from the neighboring Dutch-settled town of Store Magleby. These earlier immigrations, however, were of an essentially different kind. With one major exception, these immigrants contributed little new to the culture content but tended, rather, to be absorbed rapidly and to become indistinguishable from older Dragorians. This was possible because the migrants came in small numbers relative to the size of the community, and because they made a break with their former homes.[1] The exception is the Dutch immigrants, who came in relatively large numbers in the seventeenth and eighteenth centuries and retained their contacts with their fellow Dutch Amagerians. As a result Dragor acquired Dutch characteristics. The twentieth-century immigration was, on the other hand, one of vital, everyday intercourse—of massive social interaction. This provided the demographic base for extensive sociocultural change.

The year 1907, at which time Dragor and Copenhagen were joined by the railroad, may be taken as the date marking the end of the old era and the beginning of the new. The subsequent change constituted a social and cultural revolution, for it occurred rapidly and pervasively within the time span of a single generation. That it occurred with a general lack of cultural conflict appears to be due first of all to the fact that, in almost every citable instance, change did not involve the replacement of long-established culture patterns by radically new ones. Instead, new patterns were developed out of the old or grafted on to them. This merging of the old and the new cushioned Dragorians particularly during the early phases of urban contact and permitted a relatively easy adjustment of the people to concomitant change. Old patterns offered Dragorians a firm foothold while they grappled with the new.

This may be illustrated, both as regards their exposure to new technological exigencies as well as to changes of a strictly social order. In terms of the former adjustment, for example, eventual addition of motors was to only slightly modified versions of the old boats, and fishing traps and nets remained largely the same with only the manner of their employment changed. For all the differences that steamships implied, the old hierarchy of command and the experience of voyaging at sea remains similar in maritime employment. The job of piloting, despite advances, is essentially still to keep the craft in navigable waters. The work of Dragor's few farmers is simplified by the use of tractors and the absence of cattle, but the seasons of plowing, sowing, and harvesting were

---

[1] This process seems similar to that defined as cultural crystallization by George M. Foster in *Culture and Conquest: America's Spanish Heritage*, Viking Fund Publications in Anthropology No. 27 (New York: Wenner-Gren Foundation for Anthropological Research, 1960), 227–34.

not altered. The great development of wage labor, and the disappearance of a semisubsistence economy represent primarily the increased participation of the population in what was originally only a variant of local economic life. The few who participated in a purely money-wage economy at the turn of the century paved the way for the masses.

Technological and economic changes aside, developments in other aspects of culture were also rooted in the retention and modification of older cultural patterns. While much of the elaboration which contributed a local stamp to the annual cycle of fêtes in Dragor has been leveled out of existence with urban contact, there was always a nationally common core to their celebration and it was to this "heart" of their festivities that Dragorians could cling as an honored tradition. Much of the rites of passage, similarly derived from a common religious base, has not altered. Social organization has retained the old prestige-ordering system in new forms of hierarchical evaluation. Even sexual practices and the patterning of relations between the sexes is still founded on old principles more leniently interpreted and broadened in application.

A second and largely derived circumstance conducive to change without cultural conflict may be attributed to the harmonious system adjustments during the transitional period of the different aspects of the old Dragorian and the new urban cultures. In general, neither localized culture lag nor precocity was ever extensive enough to precipitate severe or long-felt friction.

Thus, in old Dragor with the decline in maritime employment and related businesses, the need for a shift in economic orientation was concomitant with the opening up of Copenhagen as a source of wage employment. This was a development possible only because of advances in the fields of transportation and communication—the same advances that had contributed so decisively to the economic decline of Dragor as an isolated village. Similarly, the former elaboration of the midwinter holidays, so well adjusted to a maritime economic cycle with winter inactivity, changed with urbanization to a cycle of fêtes characterized by a fairly even spacing of work-free days throughout the year and was coordinated with the growth of year-round wage labor. The addition of retirement fêtes to the rites of passage developed as old age ceased to be an almost imperceptible change in the life of an individual but became marked instead by an abrupt termination of adult economic activities.

Changes in social organization also represent harmonious adjustments to changes in economic life. The isolation of the nuclear family vis-à-vis the larger kinship groups and the disintegration of neighborhood solidarity are congruous with the increased economic independence and hence social identity of the individual and of the family unit. With technoeconomic change the old prestige and class systems became modified, to the extinction of a functioning class organization, as type of occupation, its most significant criterion, was altered. The breakdown of the church community and of the integrity of communal village government are relatable to the centrifugal tendencies of Dragor's economic ties with Copenhagen.

The cultural change within social organization had wide ramifications within other aspects of culture. With the breakdown of larger kinship groups, annual fêtes and individual celebrations have become the occasion for smaller, domestic family get-togethers or for the meeting of a few friends. Similarly the baptism rite has lost much in ceremonial magnitude and display as a result of the lack of neighborhood participation. The disappearance of the classes led to the loss of class-delineated balls and hence much of the grandeur of holiday celebrations. This relaxation of local allegiance is equally consistent with the loss of communal solidarity as evidenced here again by the declining concern with church activities and local government.

Sex life both in and outside of marriage was shown to have, within the culture of old Dragor, a functional interrelationship with coexistent patterns for defining male and female roles, the meeting of the sexes, religious attitudes, kinship behavior, and class. That is, the village's sexual practices were in support of the total cultural equilibrium of the community. While change was achieved through the familiar device of reinterpreting old patterns, sexual behavior nevertheless provides the single area in which culture conflict was discovered in conjunction with transition from village to urban status.

A third explanation of Dragor's cultural pliancy must be related to the concomitant lack of internally or externally engendered social conflict. Its only documentation was in the short-lived hostility of the youth groups to summer visitors during a few years at the turn of the century. There was no opposition of antagonistic social *groups* to encourage the exclusive adoption of either the old or the new cultural forms as symbols of a superior evaluation of culture choice. Developments were allowed to proceed solely in response to the desire of Dragorians for improved economic well-being and a higher standard of living, defined in terms comprehensible to villagers and city dwellers alike.

This lack of social conflict relates to Dragor's resolution of her technoeconomic predicament at the end of the last century without serious friction with Copenhageners. While the migration of city dwellers to Dragor was associated for some villagers with the community's loss of social and cultural integrity, the newcomers brought increased economic opportunities to that part of the population supplying goods and services locally. Further, these urban immigrants did not represent an alien group in competition with Dragorians for jobs, nor were they in a position of economic sovereignty. At that crucial period, the shift by Dragorians to an urban-oriented way of life came as a welcome palliative to an economically depressed village.

That the change to urban modes was prestigeful constitutes a fourth and last factor favoring smooth transition. A high evaluation of the city way of life was partially an adjustment to the inevitable, a product of the contemporary successful competition of Dragorians within the urban economy through conformance to urban culture patterns. But it is also strongly relatable to the ease with which one can identify with a group regarded as economically and socially privileged. This high evaluation resides additionally in Copenhagen's historical supremacy in so many areas of activity. It was the center of government, home of the king as well as the parliament, of commerce and industry, of cultural activities, of the church hierarchy, and so on. The spread of urban values was swiftest and most thorough, however, with the younger generation and is here perhaps attributable to the attendance of all Dragorian children at a single, nationally supervised school. The urban values of textbooks, of the teachers, who have almost unanimously been of nonlocal origin, as well as of children of immigrant urban families influenced the values of all Dragorian children during their formative years. This uniform motivation toward acceptance of urban culture was decisive during the early years of the century, and the adults of today who were children then reinforce these convictions in their children.

This shift in values goes far to explain those many changes which strike the eye, and yet seem avoidable. Here change appears significant for its symbolic function in the adaptive situation. On the whole, we find that village-centered diversions and local variations of nationally observed holidays and rites were abandoned. For example, children no longer set out wooden shoes for *askefis* on New Year's Eve. *Kis* is not played on Christmas Eve. Wedding celebrants do not serpentine though the village. The society balls are gone and with them a constellation of related custom. The local black confirmation costumes have been done away with to adopt the white dress of the city. These changes, negligible in terms of culture content, were exceedingly significant socially for they represent the negation of group symbols, traits that branded Dragorians as villagers, different from city people. In their place, urban symbols, such as the decorative Christmas trolls, the small-group party, and public entertainment were substituted.

In sum, the urban assimilation of Dragor was a massive process. It involved major changes in the social and cultural entity. It took place in a relatively short period of time. Dragor stands, however, a witness to the fact that abrupt, major change can take place with a minimum of social disorganization and of cultural conflict.[2]

[2] This chapter was written before the authors had seen Margaret Mead's analysis of rapid, massive, and relatively frictionless cultural change among the Manus. Dragor is similar to her Melanesian case insofar as it too suggests that short-term, all-inclusive change can be a smoother process than change of lesser scope. Cf. Margaret Mead, *New Lives for Old: Cultural Transformation—Manus, 1928–1953* (New York: New American Library, 1961), pp. 372–77.

Bibliography

Anderson, Robert T. and Barbara Gallatin Anderson. "The Timing Mechanism in Culture Lag Reduction: Changing Kinship in a Danish Community," *Kroeber Anthropological Society Papers* (Fall, 1958), 87–101.

Bobè, Louis. "Amager," *Holland-Danmark,* I, ed. by Knud Fabricius, *et al.* Copenhagen: Jespersen og Pios, 1945.

Nicolaisen, Christian. *Dragørs Fortid og Fremme.* Copenhagen: Rasmussen og Olsens, 1887.

——————. *Amagers Historie, bilagt med de vigtigste breve og aktstykker om øens forhold.* 3 vols. Copenhagen: Nordisk (vol. 1) and Schous (vols. 2 and 3), 1907, 1909, 1915.

Olsen, Gunnar. "Landbruget," *Holland-Danmark,* I, ed. by Knud Fabricius, *et al.* Copenhagen: Jespersen og Pios, 1945.

Mygdal, Elna. *Amagerdragter Vævninger og Syninger* (Danmarks Folkeminder No. 37), Copenhagen: Schønbergske, 1932.

Strunge, Mogens. *Jernskiægs Amagerrim 1963.* Copenhagen: Levin og Munksgaard, 1935.

——————. *De Thurah og Hans Amagerbog fra 1758.* Copenhagen: Levin og Munksgaard, 1936.

Trap, J. P. *Kongeriget Danmark.* (Københavns Amt, II, 4th rev. ed.) Copenhagen: G. E. C. Gads, 1929.

Zibrandtsen, Jan. *Den Hollandke Kultur paa Amager.* Copenhagen: 1938.

Index